THERE IS NO BAD BEHAVIOR THAT YOU MUST
"LEARN TO LIVE WITH."
EVERY CAT CAN BE WELL TRAINED
AND CAN BECOME A SOFT, PURRING LAPFUL OF LOVE.

FIND OUT . . .

- WHY HITTING AND SPANKING *NEVER* HELP—AND THE GENTLE APPROACH THAT DOES
- THE SECRET DISCIPLINE TOOLS YOU HAVE RIGHT AT HOME
- HAND SIGNALS AND VOICE COMMANDS YOUR CAT WILL OBEY
- BEST METHODS FOR TRAVELING WITH YOUR CAT
- DESENSITIZATION TECHNIQUES FOR SHY CATS AND SCAREDY-CATS
- THE SURPRISING FACTS ABOUT DECLAWING
- SUREFIRE HELP FOR ELIMINATING ODORS AND CAT BOX ACCIDENTS
- THE TRUTH ABOUT "ATTACK CATS" AND HOW TO TURN A FIERCE FELINE INTO A PUSSYCAT
- THE REAL DEAL ABOUT HOW YOUR CAT TRAINS YOU . . . AND SOME BEHAVIOR MODIFICATION TIPS FOR THE MEOW-MANIPULATED HUMANS IN YOUR HOUSE

AND MORE!

101 TRAINING TIPS FOR YOUR CAT

QUANTITY SALES

Most Dell books are available at special quantity discounts when purchased in bulk by corporations, organizations, or groups. Special imprints, messages, and excerpts can be produced to meet your needs. For more information, write to: Dell Publishing, 1540 Broadway, New York, NY 10036. Attention: Director, Special Markets.

INDIVIDUAL SALES

Are there any Dell books you want but cannot find in your local stores? If so, you can order them directly from us. You can get any Dell book currently in print. For a complete up-to-date listing of our books and information on how to order, write to: Dell Readers Service, Box DR, 1540 Broadway, New York, NY 10036.

101 TRAINING TIPS FOR YOUR CAT

CARIN A. SMITH, DVM

A DELL TRADE PAPERBACK

A DELL TRADE PAPERBACK

Published by
Dell Publishing
a division of
Bantam Doubleday Dell Publishing Group, Inc.
1540 Broadway
New York, New York 10036

Library of Congress Cataloging in Publication Data

Smith, Carin A.
    101 training tips for your cat / Carin A. Smith.
        p.   cm.
    Includes index.
    ISBN 0-440-50567-4
    1. Cats—Training. 2. Cats—Behavior. I. Title. II. Title: One hundred one training tips for your cat. III. Title: One hundred and one training tips for your cat.
SF446.6.S58   1994
636.8—dc20   94-8637
                                                          CIP

Printed in the United States of America

Published simultaneously in Canada

November 1994

10 9 8 7 6 5 4

RRH

To the important cats in my life

Charlie-Ebenezer, Nikki, Iris, Elsie-Mae, Maxwell, Poopsie, Gilligan-Clarence-Dexter, Andy, Bobby, Tidder, Barney, Maui, Mercury, K.C. Beans, Thomas-Bonk, Megan, Frankie, Remus, Wilbur, Isidore, Yoda, Wilma, Gumby, and Alvin.

ACKNOWLEDGMENTS

Special thanks to the following people and cats for expert advice, photograph donations, or modeling:

Jay Bender and Wilma
Lynn Boroff, Advent Hill Cattery
Jane Cartwright, Bojacat Birmans
Dr. Louise Cote, National Animal Poison Control Center
Carole Hamelman, Elorac Siamese
Sue Hanson, Cat House Originals: Cat Tree
Kami Kiani, Innovative Design: Cabitat
Gayle Martz, Sherpa's Pet Trading Co.: Sherpa Bag
Dr. Terri McCalla, Animal Eye Clinic
Steve Meharg, Kelstar Inc.: Plant Top
Gillian Rice, Gillian's Jungle: Pussy Cat Pool
Eleanor Winters, Borwick Innovations: Pet Screen Door

ACKNOWLEDGMENTS

CONTENTS

INTRODUCTION

My first cat, Charlie, was a gray-and-white tabby that I got at ten years of age—several years after I'd decided to become a veterinarian. Since then, there has never been a time when I did not own a cat (or when I was not owned by cats). My sisters and I would sneak kittens home, hide them in our bedroom, and feed them secretly until our mother heard the meows and forced them out of hiding.

Now I keep only three cats—a moderate number by some standards. Every cat is special, and whether you have one or ten, this book is meant to make your life with your cats even more enjoyable.

You can find the information you need by first looking under its major topic heading. Read through the entire table of contents to get an overview of the subjects. I've cross-referenced most of the material with "see also" notes in the text.

I have alternated the use of "he" and "she" when referring to cats in this book. Although some people refer to all animals as "it," I know that your pet is not an "it" but has an identity. Alternating the gender is also my solution to avoiding stereotypes and sexist language.

The field of cat behavior is exploding with new information. This book is an effort to bring you the most accurate and helpful material available. Behaviorists disagree on many of the fine points of training and behavior, but the advice given here is agreed upon by most. More important, it has been tested on my own cats and on the hundreds of cats owned by people that I've met as a veterinarian. I owe a big thank you to every cat owner I've met, both in person and through the computer on-line world. Without their experiences this book could not have been written.

"Hello, kitty!" I said as I peered through the cage at the animal shelter. "Are you my new cat?" The small black kitten jabbed the air with her paw, trying to reach me through the bars. Which one would I choose? The cute little calico crouched in the corner? The lively gray tabby? Or that fluffy orange kitten? Which one would you choose? Let's start at the beginning.

Consider your desires before you begin your search. Will you be happier with a purebred or mixed breed? Male or female? Long- or short-hair coat? Kitten or adult?

Any cat will give you love and make a wonderful pet. Unless you have a specific interest in breeding or showing, an ordinary house cat of either sex will fill your needs. They come in all shapes, sizes, colors, and temperaments.

Whether you want a long-haired beauty or a sleek short-haired cat, you can find a cat you will love at your local humane society or animal shelter. Also check newspaper ads and the grocery bulletin board. If you are looking for a specific color, hair length, or sex, give the shelter a list of your desires and your phone number. Ask to be notified should a kitten like that appear.

Looking for a specific breed of cat? Call your local cat fancier's club to get a show schedule. Attend a show and chat with the breeders to learn all you can about each breed. Read cat magazines to become even more familiar with purebred cats. Contact the Cat Fancier's Association for more information. (See appendix for address.)

Each breed has a particular temperament, so don't just buy on looks alone. You may be attracted to a cat's looks, but you must live with its personality. Persians have the reputation of being calm and quiet. Siamese are vocal and may need lots of attention. Abyssinians are known for their intelligence. Although there are exceptions, it is smart to assume that a cat of a

Bojacat Nadia Catmaneche, a Seal Point Birman
(Photo courtesy of Bojacat Birmans)

certain breed is more likely to have that breed's typical temperament than not.

Kittens tend to have personalities similar to their parents. Describe the type of temperament you want so the breeder can help make the best match between you and the kitten.

Buy a kitten from an established breeder who guarantees its health. You should expect to pay several hundred dollars for a pet-quality purebred cat. Breeding stock costs far more. If you get a "good deal" on a purebred, chances are that it has some kind of problem. Although it may make a fine pet, it should be neutered. Avoid the temptation to reproduce an inferior example of the breed (even though your cat is exemplary in *your* eyes!). It's not fair to others to offer anything but the best, since there is an overabundance of all kinds of cats.

ADOPTING YOUR SPECIAL CAT

Your choice of a kitten determines how well he fits into your home and how happy you are with him as an adult cat. Take some time to consider your desires, and choose a kitten based on age, personality, and—last—looks.

Do you want a quiet lap cat or a feisty playmate? A tortoiseshell or tabby? Long-haired cats are pretty but they require daily brushing. Do you have dark-colored furniture? Then a white kitten may create extra work. Do you have small children? Be sure the kitten is tolerant of being handled frequently without scratching or biting.

The best kitten for a household filled with children and other pets is one that is healthy, bold, and curious, yet allows itself to be held and petted without fuss. The quiet or shy kitten will do

*Mt. Kittery Henry of Advent Hill and Advent Hill Arctic Cat,
two Maine Coon cats
(Photo courtesy of Advent Hill Cattery)*

*Elorac Orphan Annie, a Blue Lynx Point Siamese
(Photo courtesy of Elorac Siamese)*

best as the only pet of a single person or couple. Be careful, though—the quietest kitten of a litter could be sick.

Any kitten will be playful, but all should allow themselves to be held and petted without becoming agitated. A kitten that is not used to being handled will need lots of attention and may not ever be friendly with strangers. That kitten is not a good choice for children, for people who work long hours, or for people who entertain guests frequently. (See "Wild Cats as Pets.")

What's the best age to get a kitten? Kittens learn social behavior and interactions at specific ages. If kittens have positive experiences with other animals and people at these critical ages, they happily interact with people and other animals as adults.

The ideal kitten-rearing environment is one where the kittens are handled frequently by different people during their first few months of life, yet they are left with their mother and littermates and not taken to new homes until they are three months old.

Do you want your cat to be friendly with guests and comfortable with children? Kittens that are regularly handled by a variety of people starting when they are five weeks old become cats that are comfortable around strangers. Since children look different from adults, it is best that the kitten is exposed to people of all ages.

Do you want a kitten that will get along with your other cat or dog? Kittens that are exposed to other cats and dogs during their first three months of life are comfortable with them in later life. Kittens taken away from their mother or littermates before twelve weeks of age may not get along with other cats.

Kittens learn correct behavior, including how to use the litter box, how to groom themselves, and how to eat, from their mother. They learn how to socialize with other cats by playing with their littermates. Kittens teach each other how to play fairly and how to control the intensity of biting and scratching.

If you leave a kitten with its mother until it is eight to twelve weeks old, it will grow up to be a well-adjusted cat that gets along with other cats. Avoid adopting kittens younger than eight weeks. They may be cute, but they are not ready to leave home yet. Give them time to learn to be cats.

What if you have fallen in love with an orphaned or stray kitten? Kittens that are weaned too early or are found on the street can also make good pets. But you don't know how they were handled or whether they were exposed to other cats. They need a little more attention and may not adjust as quickly to new environments, other pets, or children. As adults, these cats may be overly timid or aggressive.

You can tell a lot about a kitten even if you don't know its history. This is the case for most kittens at the animal shelter. Does the kitten approach your wiggling fingers or chase a string that you offer? Does it relax and allow itself to be held and petted without biting or scratching? Does it play happily with the other kittens? If all the answers are yes, then the kitten is likely to be well adjusted.

Should you get one kitten or two? Many people prefer two cats. There is little extra effort required. The two can keep each other company. Adopting two kittens at once avoids the problem of introducing a new kitten later when your first cat is older. (See "Introducing Cats.")

What about adopting a grown cat? Thousands of adult cats are left at animal shelters each year. Some cats' owners don't have time for them any more. Other cats' owners move somewhere that won't allow pets. And a few cats have behavior problems that their owners couldn't resolve.

Adopting an adult cat can be challenging and rewarding. Adults are less tolerant of change and have ingrained behavior patterns. Yet their mischievous kittenhood has passed. They may be the best choice for you if you don't want to endure kitten adolescence.

Adult cats are best adopted into a home without other pets. If you do have other pets, it is important to know the new cat's history. Be sure the cat has lived with other cats and dogs before.

Whether you want a cat or kitten, look closely for signs of illness. If you spot problems, you must decide if you want to take on the expense of treatment.

Does the kitten have a good appetite? Does it play with the other kittens, or hang back in a corner (possibly because it is ill)?

Check the ears for brown exudate (ear mites). Check the rear end for signs of diarrhea (parasites or intestinal virus). Look for discharge or crustiness on the eyes or nose (respiratory virus). Examine the skin, especially around the head, for bald spots, scabs, or scratches (ringworm, fleas). Ruffle the coat and look for fleas.

What if you fall in love with a kitten that may be sick? Respiratory viruses, ear mites, and ringworm are contagious. A sick kitten could spread disease. Think twice if you have other pets. Can you isolate the sick kitten until it has been completely treated? Are you willing to treat your other pets for the same illness?

Many kittenhood illnesses are minor, and you may find a hidden treasure in that quiet little kitten. Sometimes you can reduce a minor problem before you bring the kitten home. For instance, if you find fleas or flea dirt, don't bring the cat home until you have applied flea spray and combed the fleas out with a flea comb. Yet if the kitten has an irreversible illness, such as leukemia, you should find out immediately to avoid unnecessary expense and heartache.

Consider whether you are willing to pay the vet bills and whether you have the time to care for a sick kitten. If so, take the kitten directly to the vet to find out what it will take to nurse it back to health.

ADOPTION SUCCESS: FIRST DAY AT HOME

Whether you are getting your first cat or are adding another to your household, take a moment to prepare your home for the new arrival. Every cat needs a bedroom, bathroom, dining room, and playroom. Of course you won't set aside an entire room for each activity, but you need to consider areas for each of your cat's needs.

Where will your cat sleep? If not with you, then you will need to purchase or make a kitty bed. Cats prefer a cozy space elevated off the ground or tucked in a corner, away from noisy or high-traffic areas. A pillow in a basket works well.

The cat's toilet area needs careful attention. You will need a litter box, cat litter, and a scooper. Consider a covered box to contain odors and mess. The best cat litters are "dust-free" or sandlike litters. Some people use alfalfa pellets, while others prefer deodorized cat litter. Cats can be very picky about their litter. Once you choose a litter type and your cat uses it willingly, then use that litter consistently.

Now turn your attention to your cat's dining area. Your cat needs food and water bowls. Stainless steel or porcelain dishes are better than plastic, since plastic holds odors and germs. Each pet needs its own dishes.

When dogs share the house, the cat dishes must be out of the dog's reach. One handy place for the cats to eat is the top of your washer or dryer. Another option is to get a child's gate that blocks a room off from the dog but that allows the cat to jump over.

Purchase some of the same food that the cat has been fed previously. Even if you don't plan to feed it forever, you will need to mix the old food with the new food until kitty adjusts.

What about your cat's play area? Unless you provide toys and a scratching post, your kitten will make your furniture and knickknacks into playthings. Ready yourself for the onslaught of kittenhood by purchasing a few toys. Or save money by using wadded-up paper balls for toys and building your own scratching post.

Make it easy for your new cat to find necessities to avoid house soiling or furniture destruction. Put the cat's bed, scratching post, food, and litter box all in one room that you can close off temporarily. It is best to use the same room that you plan to use permanently for the litter box. Close the cat in her room each night and whenever you are away from home until you are certain she will stay out of trouble. (See "Discipline and Disobedience.")

Get a collar and ID tag for your new cat. Then shop for a cat carrier. A simple fold-away cardboard carrier is sufficient for trips to the vet. This will last for years, is much safer than a plain cardboard box, and is a preferable alternative to carrying the cat in your arms. (Even the calmest cat can be scared into scratching or running away by the sudden appearance of a big dog!) If you travel often, choose a molded plastic carrier that allows a little more room.

Now you are ready to "cat-proof" your house. Think of your kitten as you would a two-year-old child. Pretend you are a kitten looking for fun. What looks like a toy? The dangling curtain cord? The stereo wires? How about the needle and thread on the sewing machine table?

Move breakables out of kitten-jumping range. Gather up excess length in any electrical cords and band it together with a wire twist. Be sure your kitchen and bathroom trash cans have lids. Check your window screens for a snug fit.

Check your poisonous-plant list. Put dangerous plants in plant hangers out of the kitten's reach. Be sure your prescription medicines and vitamins are safely put away with lids securely fastened.

You're ready! Now you can bring your new kitten home to a safe, fun house that's equipped for her every need. But don't expect instant gratitude. The kitten may decide she would rather hide in the closet than come out to play. Give her a day or two to adjust and explore on her own. Curiosity will prevail, and soon your kitten will be looking for fun.

Show the kitten her food bowl and litter pan as soon as you bring her home. Then take her to the litter pan several times each day to be sure she doesn't forget. Close the kitten in the room with her litter pan at night until you are sure she uses it consistently.

No matter where you get your new cat or kitten, take her to your veterinarian within a few days of bringing her home. (Take her there immediately if you have other cats.) Bring a fresh stool sample with you. The kitten will be checked for health problems, vaccinated, and dewormed if necessary.

Sit down with all your family members to decide the "kitty house rules." Then stick to them. Will kitty be allowed on the dining room table? Is this an indoor cat, or will she be allowed outdoors? Who will feed the cat? No matter what your decisions, your cat will be happiest if she has consistent rules and a consistent schedule.

ALLERGIES TO CATS

Are you one of thousands of cat lovers who is allergic to cats? If so, you are not alone. Keeping cats in a home where someone is allergic is a lot of work. Some people are so allergic they can't keep cats. Yet many others have devised ways to keep cats in their lives without becoming miserable.

Control of your allergy starts with your own physician. Medication or allergy shots may be given. But you also can do a lot in your home to reduce the problem.

Your cat should never be allowed in your bedroom. (See

"Sleeping.") Keep the rest of your house spotless with daily vacuuming and dusting. Get rid of carpets wherever you can, since carpeting collects and holds allergens.

Use a whole-house humidifier and an air purifier to keep dust and hair down. Change the filter in your forced-air system frequently. Keep furniture clean with a lint remover. Wash your hands after handling your cat. Wash your hands and change your clothes after grooming the cat.

Bathe your cat weekly to remove loose hair and dander. You may not need to shampoo the cat, but just to wet him. Experts recommend using distilled water. Commercial "antiallergy" products can be sprayed on the cat's coat to help reduce your reaction.

You may be allergic to cat saliva, hair, or dander (small scales from the skin and hair). The type of cat you own may affect your allergic reaction. Some people react more to long-haired cats than short-haired ones, or vice versa. Several breeds of cats with unusual coats may be less allergenic than others.

The Devon Rex and Cornish Rex have only an undercoat and no "guard hairs," the outer coat found on other cats. The Japanese Bobtail is said to shed less than other cats. The Sphynx cat is practically bald, but has very oily skin that might cause more problems than the lack of hair solves. Owning one of these cats won't guarantee that you don't have an allergic reaction, but some people report that they react less.

*Altering your cat will reduce his or her urge
to wander in search of romance.*

ALTERING YOUR CAT

Spay surgery is done to females, and castration is done to males. A spay is an *ovariohysterectomy*—the removal of the uterus and ovaries. A castration is an *orchiectomy*—the removal of the testicles. Some people use the word *neuter* to apply only to castration, while others use it to apply to both spay and castration. A "neuter" is a cat of either sex that has had its gonads removed.

Altering your cat eliminates its ability to reproduce. Removing the sexual organs also removes the sexual urges and hormonal swings that occur in intact cats.

The incidence of breast cancer is about seven times greater in queens (intact females) than in spayed females. What's more, most of the behavior of sexually intact cats is objectionable to people. Both tomcats and queens will wander more if let outdoors.

A female in heat has obnoxious, loud behavior. She meows constantly, rubs against you, rolls on the floor, and makes a nuisance of herself. Like intact male cats, females in heat sometimes spray urine. Many cat owners present a cat to the vet when her in-heat behavior is mistakenly interpreted as a sign of distress.

Females remain in heat for ten to fourteen days. If the cat doesn't get pregnant, she will return to heat in two to three weeks. If she does get pregnant (which usually occurs, despite your precautions), you must pay for the kittens' vaccinations and deworming, then find homes for them all. Often the cat gets pregnant again so quickly you miss getting her spayed and the cycle repeats. A female in heat will attract tomcats that fight and urinate on your property, creating awful noise and odors.

The tomcat sprays urine to mark his territory. He fights with other cats and develops constant abscesses that need veterinary treatment. He yowls all night when a female is near. Unless you are keeping a stud cat specifically for breeding, leaving a tomcat intact only makes him frustrated.

There is no medical or psychological need for your cat to reproduce. Cats that are spayed before their first heat have no deficiencies of any kind. In fact, cats gain the most health benefits by being spayed before their first heat. If you want your children to watch the miracle of birth, ask your veterinarian to show them a videotape of kittens being born.

Neutering will not make your cat fat. Lack of exercise and too much food make him fat. Since your neutered cat won't spend all his energy looking for romance, you should give him something else to do to occupy his time. Play with him.

Although it is best to have your cat altered before he reaches puberty, many of the benefits of neutering occur no matter what the cat's age. For instance, there is a 90 percent chance that your tomcat's fighting or urine-spraying will stop *no matter what his age when he is neutered.*

Traditionally, spaying and castrating were recommended at six months of age. More recently, cats have been altered at much younger ages—as early as two months. The main reason for early surgery is that it can be done before a pet is adopted. That prevents the new pet owner from "forgetting" to neuter a pet or deciding not to neuter after initially agreeing to do so (an unfortunately common occurrence).

Castration and spay surgeries carry low risk and have few complications. Your cat is anesthetized so he cannot feel anything. Modern anesthetics are extremely safe.

Two incisions are made in the male cat's scrotum. The testicles are removed and the blood vessels are tied off to prevent bleeding. Absorbable stitches are used or the vessel is tied to itself, so you don't have to take the cat back for suture removal. You must take away your cat's usual litter for a few days so the granules don't irritate the incision. Use shredded paper instead.

The spay operation is a bit more involved. The cat's abdomen is opened so the uterus and ovaries can be removed. Internal absorbable stitches tie off the blood vessels and close the abdominal wall. Some veterinarians place stitches in the skin that must be removed later, while others use only subcutaneous (under the skin) stitches that absorb by themselves.

Although the spay surgery is a routine one, it is still major abdominal surgery. Your cat should stay indoors for a week afterward so the incision stays clean and dry. If your cat was in heat, she may still act as if in heat and will still attract males for a week or so.

Most cats feel little discomfort after the surgery. Your vet can give your cat an injection for pain if you are concerned. Yet you may be envious of how little your cat notices its surgery. Most cats are back to normal within two days. Complete healing takes two weeks.

Are there any advantages to *not* neutering your pet? Few, if any, exist. Some people worry that neutering will increase their male cat's chances of developing urinary tract blockage. We now know that blockages are related to the diet's acidity and mineral content, so there is no reason to avoid neutering male cats.

You can watch kittens being born on a videotape. You can play with kittens or adopt new ones at your local animal shelter. And if you're avoiding the surgery out of concern for your cat, remember that he will fight more often, feel frustrated much of the time, and continually wander off in search of romance. That means higher vet bills, an unhappy cat, and the risk of losing your cat altogether.

ALTERNATIVE MEDICINE:
ACUPUNCTURE, HOMEOPATHY,
NATURAL THERAPY

Some people turn to alternative medicine only after traditional methods have failed. Others use alternative methods as their first choice. Either way, it is important to understand what methods are available and what they really can and cannot do to help your cat.

The problem with most nontraditional approaches is that they have few regulations or standards. Shysters make a fortune on catchy words, false hopes, and diseases without a cure. The best advice is "buyer beware."

Alternative medicine includes the use of natural and herbal medications, acupuncture, holistic medicine, and homeopathic medicine. Many people throw these words around without a true understanding of their meanings.

Chances are that everyone would prefer to use *natural, organic, or herbal* treatments if they worked as well as artificial chemicals. Unfortunately, no labeling laws protect you from inappropriate use of these words on pet products.

You must become a label sleuth, searching the fine print for information. What ingredients are "natural," and how are they obtained? What is it about that herbal ingredient that makes it superior? Beware of paying extra for variations of ordinary medications just because they're labeled "organic."

Natural or herbal remedies can be overdosed or cause side effects, just like any medication. Using the plant itself, rather than a pill or injection, does not change the fact that you are putting a foreign substance into your cat.

Acupuncture is an accepted part of modern medicine. Needles are used to stimulate acupuncture points, each of which has a specific effect on the body. Acupuncture's best use is in management of chronic pain.

Acupuncture must be done by a veterinarian who has first diagnosed the problem to be treated. The veterinarian should be certified by the International Veterinary Acupuncture Society.

Holistic refers to the entire body and its surroundings. A veterinarian practicing holistic medicine considers illness as a product of the cat's environment.

Some people use the word *holistic* to refer to all alternative treatment. Holistic medicine, though, refers to a specific approach that may include alternative or traditional therapy. Any good veterinarian practices holistic medicine without labeling it as such.

For example, a cat with asthma often must be treated with drugs. Yet a big part of treatment is identifying irritants in the home, such as cigarette smoke, and eliminating those. That means the vet must take a holistic approach and inquire about the cat's environment, looking beyond blood tests and X rays.

Homeopathic medicine operates under the theory that diseases may be treated with substances that would ordinarily cause signs of that same disease in a healthy individual. The substances are given in tiny doses to the sick patient.

Homeopathic medicine is a part of mainstream practice, although few "traditional" veterinarians would label their methods as such. For instance, vaccination works by injecting small amounts of a disease-causing agent to stimulate the animal's own immunity. The vaccine may contain just a part of the organism or a killed organism, so that it cannot cause disease itself.

Other uses of homeopathic medicine are not as commonly used. There is no reason to believe that *every* ailment can be treated with a homeopathic approach, and in fact that approach could be harmful or useless in many cases. Before you blithely use that homeopathic treatment, be sure you know what substance you are using, what it does, and its side effects.

Realize that some veterinarians who practice "alternative medicine" may not even describe themselves that way. Others just use the labels as a marketing gimmick to get your business. When someone says he or she uses a form of alternative medicine, ask what that means. Don't just assume the words mean the same to you both.

Rather than looking for a specific type of alternative therapy, search for a veterinarian whose approach is thorough and open-minded, and who uses both "alternative" and traditional medicine when each is necessary. Look for a veterinarian who examines your cat carefully, stresses prevention over treatment, and considers your cat's environment when treatment is necessary.

APPETITE LOSS

Has your cat lost his appetite? Although cats can be finicky, they usually eat enough to keep healthy. Something is wrong when a cat doesn't eat. Kitty is either stressed or sick. Sometimes the problem is as simple as a new food the cat doesn't like. If that's the case, mix some of the old food in with the new until kitty accepts the change. (See "Feeding Finicky Cats.")

A new addition to the family, a new pet, or a move to a new home could create enough stress to cause your cat to stop eating. Certain breeds, such as the Siamese, are more sensitive and prone to anorexia nervosa, a nervous loss of appetite.

Has a change in your cat's life caused him to stop eating? You may need to give kitty extra attention for several weeks until he comes to accept the change in your home. Cats need to eat in a place that is quiet and free from distractions. Try taking your cat somewhere that is quiet and cozy.

Many cats eat better if they are stroked and talked to while they eat. Sometimes your cat will eat small pieces of food out of your hand when he won't eat out of the bowl. Sit with your cat and talk to him to encourage him to eat. Offer him a little treat, maybe some yogurt or tuna, to show him he's special.

Cats also don't eat when they are sick and have a fever. If your cat stops eating or loses his appetite for more than a few days, take him to the vet for a checkup.

Most of the time your cat will recover quickly from whatever caused his drop in appetite. The appetite problem doesn't need to be treated, because once the illness goes away, the appetite automatically returns. But sometimes a longer illness takes hold and kitty's poor appetite becomes a problem. Often the illness itself requires that a special diet be fed and that certain foods are off-limits. What can you do to stimulate your cat's appetite?

Offer food several times daily. Try both canned and dry food and offer different flavors. Leave the food out only for thirty minutes or as long as kitty is eating, then take it up again. Refrigerate canned food in between meals. Cats may not eat canned food that has been sitting out in a dish for several hours. What's more, the food could become spoiled.

Heat canned food in the microwave to release its odors. Adding a strong flavor or smell also can help stimulate the appetite. Try these flavor additions:

- Water from water-packed tuna (eat the tuna yourself)
- Clam juice
- Garlic powder
- Meat-flavored baby food

If your cat is eating a therapeutic diet, be sure to get your vet's okay before you make any additions. Certain supplements may be off-limits for cats with some diseases. For instance, cats with heart disease cannot have salty foods and cats with kidney failure cannot have much added protein.

Ask your vet if it is appropriate to use Nutrical, a high-calorie vitamin supplement. This gooey paste tastes very good. If your cat is not eating well at all, try mixing a bit of Nutrical with some baby food to get him to eat. You can put some of this on your finger and wipe it off into your cat's mouth. Although you shouldn't rely on Nutrical more than a few days, sometimes that's enough to get his taste buds reactivated and interested. (See "Weight Loss" for more tips.)

ATTACKING PEOPLE

Rowdy's owner grimly revealed the scratches on her arm. "I love this cat," she said, "but her attacks are getting ferocious! It's as if she thinks I'm a scratching post. The only time she is nice is when she's sleeping. Is there any hope for changing her behavior?"

A cat that attacks people is going one step beyond biting or scratching when handled. (Read "Biting, Scratching, and Clawing People" for more tips.) You must determine the cause of the aggression before you can stop the behavior. Consider when the behavior occurs and how you respond. Watch the cat's body language to determine if she is playing, angry, or defensive. If you have difficulty solving a problem on your own, ask your veterinarian for advice. Don't risk getting yourself or another person injured. For tips on cats that attack other cats, see "Fighting Cats."

A cat that pounces on or attacks you may be exhibiting *play aggression.* This behavior includes biting, scratching, and pouncing. A cat that is the only cat in a household is most likely to show play aggression. The aggression is directed more at the cat's owners than at strangers.

Cats that attack people when they are moving may be play-hunting. For instance, one cat would hide next to the staircase and attack her owner's feet when he walked by. Play aggression can seem like a serious attack at times. Just because it is "play" doesn't mean that it is appropriate behavior.

Learned aggression occurs when a cat learns that she can make you do something by biting or attacking you. For instance, one cat would claw at her owner's pants every time she wanted to be picked up. In another case, a child continually pulled a cat's tail. The cat would strike out in pain, causing the child to stop. Later the cat began to strike at the child *before* her tail was pulled.

To prevent either learned aggression or play aggression, create an unpleasant experience for your cat when she does the bad behavior. Hands-on physical punishment won't work because the cat may strike back at you. Instead, squirt your cat with a sharp blast of water or make a loud noise *every time* she attacks or bites you. Your reaction must be instant for best results, so you may need to carry your water bottle or foghorn with you for a time. Never reward the behavior by petting, picking up, or feeding your cat.

Punishment alone won't work for playful cats. Cats with play aggression also need to have their energy redirected by giving them toys. (Giving a cat a toy is redirecting, not rewarding her behavior; see "Biting, Scratching, and Clawing People.") Moving toys such as a ball or fishing pole toy help divert cats that like to pounce on moving people. *Never play with the cat using your hands.*

Collect several stuffed mice, foam balls, or wadded-up paper balls. Keep these soft toys in your pocket so you can react instantly when your cat attacks you. Immediately throw a toy at the cat so she redirects her attack toward the toy. Sometimes you can predict when your cat will attack. For instance, if your cat always attacks you when you come down the stairs, throw a ball down just before you come. Eventually your cat will learn to attack the toy, not you, in the first place.

Play aggression is also helped by getting another cat for yours to play with. Getting another cat automatically provides your cat with a natural outlet for her energy.

Cats also may be aggressive when frightened or trapped. The cat's "critical distance" is the distance that unknown people can approach before she feels threatened. If the cat can escape, she does so before the person gets that close. But if she feels trapped, she may strike out.

The solution here is to give the cat a better opportunity to escape and to avoid invading her personal space. That is not always possible, though. For instance, a cat may need to have a veterinary exam. Veterinarians usually use a towel to get a safe hold on an aggressive patient.

Cats that were not socialized to people at an early age may not tolerate anyone but their owners. If your cat is hostile toward strangers, shut her in a room with her food and litter box when you expect guests. This is not "locking her out" but giving her a secure, quiet place to relax without being forced to face strangers. See "Shy, Timid, or Fearful Cats" for more tips.

Another type of aggression is transferred or redirected to you from whatever causes your cat's anger. For instance, your cat sees another cat through the screen door. The two exchange angry howls and hisses, and then you walk by. Your cat is so upset she strikes out at the nearest thing—you.

Try to eliminate the cause of your cat's anger if this happens. If you can't get rid of the stray cat (see "Stray Cats"), try to block your cat's view of the invader. But be careful—if you try to calm your cat or interfere when she is aroused, you could be attacked. Avoid close contact with your cat when she is angry.

There also can be medical reasons for a cat's aggression. Any sick cat will be irritable. A cat that is in pain may lash out when you try to pick her up. Both hyperthyroid and hypothyroid conditions can cause a cat to become irritable. Of these, hyperthyroidism is far more common. It usually occurs in cats older than about eight years.

Because aggression can have many causes, you should be careful that you are using the appropriate training method for your cat's problem. For instance, a cat with transferred aggression won't be helped by getting a second cat. Yet a cat with play aggression could improve when another kitten is brought home.

Much more is known about aggression than can be discussed here. Always get expert advice if there is any chance your cat could harm someone. If you aren't sure why your cat is acting aggressively, consult a veterinarian or behavior specialist. That way you can use the technique that will give you the best results for your cat's problem.

BAD BREATH

Your cat, George, jumps on the back of the couch and rubs his cheek against yours. You start to rub back when you get a whiff of his breath—phew! What could his problem be?

You may find the cause of your cat's bad breath by looking in his mouth. First lift the cat's lip on one side of the jaw. You don't have to open the mouth at all. Just lift the lip far back enough that you can see the sides of the rear teeth. Are they white or brown? Look at the gum line where it meets the teeth. Is there a red line along the border?

Redness along the gum line is a sign of gingivitis—inflammation of the gums. Brown deposits on the teeth are tartar. If you see either of these problems, you should make an appointment with your vet to have your cat's teeth cleaned.

It is important that you have teeth cleaning done at a veterinary office that uses an ultrasonic cleaner and polisher. Simply scraping the tartar off the teeth may seem sufficient, but the tartar will return faster and worse than before. That's because scraping the teeth leaves tiny grooves in the enamel that collect tartar. All surfaces of all the teeth must be cleaned and polished thoroughly, and that is possible only by anesthetizing the cat and using a dental machine. Modern anesthetics make the process safe even for older cats.

Cats that eat canned food may accumulate food in between the teeth, which causes bad breath. Also, canned food seems to make cats prone to tartar buildup. Consider switching to dry food to eliminate these problems.

What if your cat's teeth are pearly white but his breath still stinks? Take a closer look at his mouth. Grasp his head with one hand. Place your thumb on the upper jaw just under his eye on one side and your fingers on the opposite upper jaw. Use one finger of your other hand to hinge open his lower jaw. Open it only enough to see, since your cat will resent your stretching his jaw too far.

Look closely at the tongue and the back of the throat. Are there any red spots, lumps, or sores? If so, you should have a veterinarian examine your cat.

Bad breath may occur with no signs at all in the cat's mouth. Your cat could have gotten into the trash or something rotten outdoors. There are kitty mouthwashes you can get for short-term problems. (Don't use a "people" mouthwash.) However, if your cat's bad breath lasts more than a few days, have your vet take a look to be sure there isn't something wrong.

BATHING

Some cats love baths, some tolerate them, and some won't endure them. You probably assume your cat is in that last category. In reality most cats do tolerate bathing quite well. You have two choices: Do it yourself or take the cat to a groomer. Groomers are expert at bathing cats and they charge a minimal fee.

When does a cat need a bath? Not often. Show cats are bathed frequently to look their best, but your house cat grooms herself quite nicely. Cats don't require regular baths, but occasionally they will get into something odorous, sticky, or dirty.

Proper preparation is the key to a successful cat bath. Get your kitty shampoo, plastic cup, washcloth, and towel together next to the tub. Use a shampoo that is labeled for cats. Cats have very sensitive skin that could become irritated with certain shampoos, soaps, or detergents.

Brush your cat first to remove loose hair. Remove mats before bathing because they will just get worse when wet.

Bathe your cat in your laundry sink, kitchen sink, or bathroom tub. It is best if the room is one that can be closed off so kitty can't escape. A sink with a spray nozzle attachment is especially convenient.

Cats don't like the sound of running water. It is easier to get the water ready before you get your cat. Run the tap water until it is exactly your skin temperature. Fill the sink or your tub a few inches deep. You want just enough water to be able to wet the cat using your cup, but not so much that the cat is swimming. If you want to wet the cat using a spray nozzle, turn it on to a slow trickle.

Now get kitty, go into the bathroom, and shut the door. This step is essential for success. You don't want the bath to turn into a chasing game.

Put a cotton ball in each of kitty's ears. Pick up your cat and place her in the tub. Do not do this slowly. Do not hold kitty close to your body, or she will try to climb up your shirt. Pick her up deliberately and place her definitively in the tub.

Hold kitty by the scruff of the neck with one hand throughout the rest of this procedure. Grasp a large handful of skin at the scruff of the neck and just hold on. Don't try to restrain your cat's legs. The more you try to hold her body, the more she will fight. Usually if you just have a good hold on the scruff she can't go anywhere. Don't lift her legs off the floor of the tub or she will fight to regain her balance.

Now use your other hand to wet the cat using your cup. If you use a spray nozzle instead, keep the water at a slow trickle and hold the nozzle close to the cat's skin.

Then apply shampoo and suds it in. Most cats will just crouch down and endure the bath. But even if kitty sits quietly, don't let go—she will bolt out of the tub in an instant. Of course, since you closed the door your only problem will be a wet bathroom.

Take the drain plug out and allow the sudsy water to drain. Face your cat away from the faucet and turn the water on slowly. Leave the stream at a slow trickle to avoid scaring your cat. Use your cup or spray nozzle to rinse off the shampoo. Be sure to rinse thoroughly, especially between the toes and under the tail.

Squeeze the water out of your cat's coat with your hands. Then pick her up, place her in a towel, and rub her dry. Keep her indoors until she is completely dry. Then brush your cat to remove loose hair.

BEGGING

Imagine you have just settled down to a romantic, candlelit dinner with your loved one. Classical music plays softly in the background. You gaze across the table and are about to utter some words of love when you feel a paw on your leg. . . . "Meow! Meow!"

You hadn't noticed how obnoxious kitty had become lately

because the usual noise and commotion of daily meals concealed the problem. You only sneak an occasional treat to kitty, but he acts as if he *always* gets fed from the table. How can you stop this behavior?

To understand your cat's behavior, you must understand something about training. "Intermittent positive reinforcement" is a great way to train your cat. That means that once you have taught a cat something, you need only give an occasional reward to encourage kitty to repeat that behavior. The chance of a reward is enough to cause the behavior to continue.

In this case you have trained your cat to beg at the table. Giving your cat a treat only once a week while you are dining teaches kitty that it is possible to get a treat when he begs. It doesn't matter that you don't do it all the time. The fact that you *ever* do so is enough to cause the begging to continue.

You must do two things to stop the begging. First, never *ever* give kitty anything while you are sitting at the table. Second, get out your noisemaker or water bottle (see "Discipline Tools"), and make the cat stop by squirting him or making a loud noise. Don't allow kitty to beg at any time—no exceptions allowed. Consistency on your part will yield faster results.

BITING, SCRATCHING, AND CLAWING PEOPLE

Does your cat bite or scratch you? You can stop the behavior if you know its cause. Cats scratch people for two main reasons: in play or in defense. Some cats go beyond biting or scratching when held and actually pounce on or attack people. (See "Attacking People.")

The tips here are for mild to moderate problems. If your cat shows potential to really injure you, get help from your veterinarian first. You may need to use a combination of medication and training to reduce your cat's aggression.

Kittens learn how much pain they can inflict by playing with their littermates. They learn how much of a bite causes a reaction and then learn to modify their play-attack. Single or orphan kittens, deprived of this experience, may not learn that they should not bite hard.

If you wrestle with your cat, she learns that it is okay to play roughly. Later she may scratch or bite you when you pet her. She feels confused when you punish her and may scratch even more if you swat her to tell her no. She doesn't know that you aren't play-wrestling any more.

To stop your cat from scratching, first you must decide never to use your hands and arms for anything except petting. If you want to play with kitty, use a toy.

Some kittens are less interested in being petted than others. Accept your cat's personality and don't force petting when it isn't invited. Most kittens appreciate petting more after they are grown. As kittens, they would rather play.

When your cat scratches you, immediately stop what you are doing. Just freeze or go limp, stopping all movement. That usually stops the stimulus that caused kitty to scratch or bite in "fun." Then put the cat down and go do something else for a while.

Another tactic is to give the cat a toy immediately when she begins her behavior. (Do the "go limp" step first, so she doesn't grab at your departing hand.) That teaches her that it is okay to be aggressive with toys, and it gives her an immediate outlet for her feelings. Keep several toys handy to give to kitty when she becomes rough. Try using balls, fishing pole toys, and large stuffed toys.

Eventually kitty will learn that when she has those playful feelings, she should attack a toy and not you. (Giving the cat a toy is not "rewarding" her. Since play behavior is a normal instinct, you must give the cat an alternative to biting you. See "Training Basics" for more.)

Cats also bite or scratch when they are restrained and want to get away. That usually happens if they are being given medicine or are held while they are frightened. To avoid being scratched when you give medicine, you need to hold the cat properly. Keep her comfortable so she has less of a desire to escape. Wrap the cat in a towel to keep her paws away. (See "Holding a Cat.")

Most cat bites and scratches happen to children. The child does something that hurts the cat, so the cat lashes out. Children must be taught the proper way to interact with a cat. Cats and children should not be left unsupervised until you are certain that no problems will arise.

Does your cat curl up on your lap to be petted, then suddenly bite your hand? Males do this more often than females. It is thought that there is a "threshold" beyond which petting is no longer acceptable. Your pet may be affectionate in other ways, but this is one habit he doesn't enjoy.

Your cat may like sitting in your lap but not being petted. Your best bet is to respect your cat's wishes. Punishment won't help. Try to learn how much petting your cat will tolerate and stop petting before that point is reached. If the problem becomes severe, your vet may prescribe medication to alter the cat's behavior.

A cat that bites you unexpectedly may be injured. If you happen to pet a painful area, the cat's natural reaction is to strike out. A cat that suddenly bites someone without apparent reason should be examined by a veterinarian.

BOARDING

Should you board your cat during your vacation? You may feel more distress when boarding your cat than the cat seems to feel. Some cats do become stressed at any disruption in their daily schedule. They will fare better at home with a cat-sitter. (See "Cat-sitter.") Yet most cats have no problems when they are boarded.

Chances are that you can find a kennel that is appropriate for your cat. Get your vet's recommendation and ask your friends where they have boarded their cats. Prepare a list of questions, then call the kennel for information.

What kind of food is fed? Can you provide your cat's own food? How often are the cats checked on weekends and holidays? What provisions are made for veterinary care if a cat should become ill? If you happen to return on a weekend, can you pick up your cat then, or do you have to wait until Monday? The kennel should require that all cats are vaccinated before they are boarded.

Visit the kennel to be sure it is clean, spacious, quiet, and odor-free. The least stressful boarding situation is one where there are no dogs or where dogs are kept in a different room. Some cat boarding kennels have deluxe kitty accommodations, with two-story "condos," raised perches, and even TV. A view of the outdoors is a plus.

Once you have checked every aspect of the kennel's operation, you can leave your cat there and enjoy your holiday without worry.

BOY OR GIRL—WHAT SEX?

The two questions that usually arise regarding gender are "What sex is my cat?" and "Which sex makes the best pet?"

You will feel slightly awkward if you name your cat Cinderella only to find out that she's a he. So let's have a short course in anatomy to clear things up.

The male cat's penis doesn't stick out as it does in other animals. You have to look at other anatomy. Lift the tail and look below the anus at the opening where the urine comes out.

The female vulva looks like a slit. The urethral opening of the male is a bit lower than the female's vulva and looks like a dot. So, when you look at both the anus and the opening below, in the female it will look like a semicolon (;) whereas in the male it will look like a colon (:).

Once a male kitten gets to be several months old, you can begin to see the scrotum. Look for two swellings just below the anus. You also can try to extrude the penis if you aren't sure. Lay the kitten on his back, and gently press down just in front of the urethral opening. This will cause the penis of a male kitten to stick out.

Sexing small kittens can be difficult, especially if you have only one kitten or if you have several of the same sex. In a mix of kittens, you can compare several and then see the small differences in the anatomy. But sometimes you just have to wait a few weeks until they get big enough to tell.

Certain coat colors can give you a clue to the cat's sex. Calico and tortoiseshell cats are usually female. Orange cats tend to be male.

Which gender makes the best pet? Some people prefer males since it costs less to neuter a male than to spay a female. Yet that cost is a tiny fraction of what you will spend in the cat's lifetime.

Males are more likely to spray urine than females, but the

incidence is low. About 10 percent of all neutered males will spray urine sometime in their lives. Spraying is more likely in a multiple-cat household.

The final say comes back to you. Cats of either sex make fine pets. Since you are likely to alter your cat, the behavior that is typical of one sex or the other will not be pronounced. More important than gender is the cat's good health and agreeable personality.

BRUSHING TEETH

What can you do to keep your cat's teeth healthy? Begin dental care when your cat is still a kitten. Feed only dry food to reduce tartar buildup. But you can't rely on dry food or on "tartar-removing" treats to keep your cat's teeth healthy. Learn to brush your cat's teeth.

Daily brushing is best, but weekly brushing is better than none at all. If you've never done so, ask your vet to show you how. Start by simply teaching your cat to allow you to handle her mouth. Some time when your cat is sitting contentedly in your lap, insert one finger under her lip and rub the outside edges of her teeth. Stop after just a few seconds and give her lots of praise.

Continue to use just your finger, and increase the time you rub your cat's teeth and gums. You don't need to open your cat's mouth at first. Just rub the outside edges of all the teeth by lifting her lip and using one finger. Rub along the line where the teeth meet the gum.

Stop *before* your cat gets irritated or restless. If you stop after your cat objects, she learns that she can make you stop. Once your cat allows you to use your finger in her mouth, wrap a small piece of gauze around your finger and do the same thing.

You may continue to use moistened gauze as your "toothbrush," get a kitty toothbrush, or use a small child's toothbrush. Whenever you switch to something new, start all over again with short sessions. Begin to rub the teeth with your finger, then insert the brush for just a short time. Give lots of praise and stop.

Ask your veterinarian for cat toothpaste. Human toothpaste is not recommended since it is made to be spit out and cats will swallow it instead. Some cats love the flavor of cat toothpaste. Put a little bit on your finger and see if your cat licks it off. If not, start by using just a tiny amount of the toothpaste to get your cat used to the flavor.

Apply the toothpaste to your gauze or toothbrush and proceed as usual. With this gradual approach you will soon be able to brush your cat's entire mouth using a toothbrush and toothpaste. Some people continue to use gauze and plain water because their cat objects too much to a brush or the flavor of toothpaste. Either way the cat's teeth will benefit.

Does your cat need to have her teeth professionally cleaned? Cats won't show signs of pain even when they have severe tooth decay. They usually continue to eat normally too.

Take a closer look. Lift the lip on the side of your cat's mouth. Look at the outside edges of the teeth that are the farthest back in the mouth. Usually these are affected the worst. A light brown film is tartar. Red gums, and black spots or white soft material on the teeth, are signs of infection. A cat that resists having her teeth looked at may be feeling pain in the mouth.

Once tartar has accumulated, the teeth must be professionally cleaned. Infected gums and decayed teeth don't take care of themselves. Although this condition is "natural" in the wild, it also contributes to a shorter life span—not to mention the discomfort the cat surely feels. Decayed teeth must be extracted or repaired. Some old cats lose almost all their teeth, but they fare well when fed soft food.

Scaling the teeth with a hand scaler is not sufficient to clean the teeth thoroughly. Veterinarians use an ultrasonic scaler and polisher just like those your dentist uses. Unfortunately, we can't tell the cat to sit still and open her mouth. Anesthesia is necessary to do a thorough job. With today's modern anesthetics, it is safe to anesthetize most cats, including the elderly. Preoperative blood tests are recommended on cats over eight to ten years old to spot any potential problems before anesthesia.

CATNIP

Catnip is one of the wonders of the cat world. Give kitty a bit of catnip to sniff, and she will become playful and happy. Rub catnip on anything you want your cat to enjoy. For instance, you can use catnip to train kitty to use a new scratching post. Rub some catnip on a new cat toy to get kitty interested in playing with it.

Dry or fresh catnip leaves and stems contain an oil that elicits the cat's response. Catnip may be hallucinogenic for cats. Long-time exposure to catnip can make a kitty seem "spaced out," or slightly unaware of her surroundings. Although the cat's response to catnip is well known, no one knows for sure what causes the reaction.

Cats usually react to catnip by chewing, rubbing in, or licking the plant. The cat's playful behavior lasts for several minutes, then the cat seems to feel euphoric for up to an hour. However, catnip doesn't cause this response in all cats: Up to one-third of

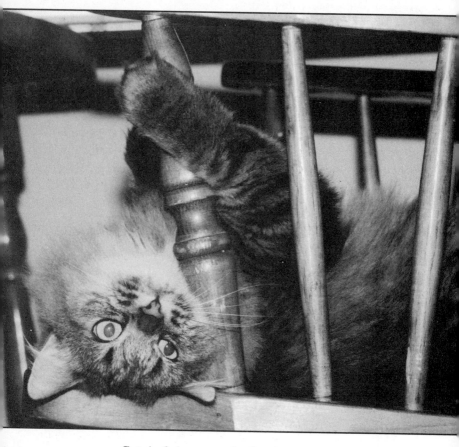

Catnip brings out the fun in your cat.

cats don't respond to catnip at all. The ability to respond to catnip appears to be inherited.

Several other plants and chemicals have been reported to cause changes in the cat's behavior. Some people have reported their cats react just as strongly to the odor of a certain shampoo or lotion. The fragrance in these products may contain a chemical that causes kitty to react.

CAT-SITTER

Hiring a cat-sitter is one of the least stressful ways to have your cat cared for in your absence. Kitty enjoys his normal home life, and you have someone checking the house every day.

When do you need a cat-sitter? Most cats fare well when left alone for a day or two. Just be certain to leave extra water bowls (in case one tips over) and lots of extra food.

You need a cat-sitter if you plan to be away more than a few days, if your cat receives medication, or if your cat suffers from separation anxiety and tends to destroy the house in your absence. Even if you could leave enough food for a week, you still should have someone check in on kitty to be sure everything is all right. Besides, you need someone to get your mail and water the plants.

You can choose a professional pet-sitter or the next-door neighbor. Teenagers and retired persons both make good pet-sitters. Find someone who can do the job regularly so your cat gets to know that person.

A neighbor or friend might offer to care for your cat for free. Yet paying the sitter allows you to ask for their services frequently without feeling guilty. It also makes them feel like they are doing a real job so they pay attention to details. You won't feel bad asking a paid pet-sitter to get the mail, water plants, and clean up your cat's mess. Another alternative is to work out a trade agreement with someone, as long as you both take vacations at different times.

With professional pet-sitters or people you don't know well, be sure to call their references. Ask specific questions, such as "Did the sitter remember to lock the house?" or "Were the food and water dishes full when you returned?" That way you will get specific information beyond "They did a good job."

Professional pet-sitters should be licensed, bonded, and have liability insurance. Ask about the specific person who will be seeing your cat and about how the employees of the pet-sitting service are chosen.

What time of day will the sitter visit your home, and how many visits per day are included with the service? If your cat is on medication, be sure that the sitter is accustomed to giving medicine to cats.

Have your cat-sitter visit your home to meet your cat and learn where food and toys are located. Watch the sitter's attitude toward your cat. Pay attention to the sitter's entry and exit —is the sitter careful enough to look for a cat nearby *before* opening the front door?

Try the sitter for a short vacation before you trust him or her with your pet for several weeks. Leave a detailed list of instructions no matter whom you hire, even if you gave verbal instructions. Don't assume that the person knows anything. List the amount of food and water to give, brand of food you prefer to feed, name and dose of any medications, and phone numbers for you and your veterinarian.

Give your veterinarian the name of your cat-sitter too. Authorize treatment of any unexpected illness.

Be sure your cat wears a collar and identification tag at all times. Both outdoor and indoor cats must have some way of being identified if they are lost or injured. In spite of everyone's best intentions, an indoor cat occasionally gets out. Put your veterinarian's or a friend's phone number on the tag in addition to your own. If you are on vacation, no one can reach you at your home phone number.

CHEWING AND SUCKING

Some cats develop an annoying habit of chewing or sucking on their owners' sweaters or other objects. Others chew or suck on themselves, their littermates, or their owners. Kittens get in trouble chewing electrical cords or drapery pulls.

Two types of sucking problems occur. One type occurs in kittens that are orphaned or are weaned too early. The kitten has a strong instinct to suck and does so on what ever convenient object may be nearby. Usually the sucking is accompanied by kneading the feet, just as a kitten does while it is nursing.

Kittens usually grow out of their sucking habit. You can discourage the sucking in the same way that a mother cat stops her kittens from nursing when it is weaning time. She swats them on the nose and says "No." You can lift the kitten by the nape of her neck, say "No," and set her down away from the object she was sucking on. A little flick of your finger on her nose is all the swat you need.

You also can try smearing or spraying bad-tasting stuff on the items that the kitten chews. Use Bitter Apple (available at pet stores) or hot pepper oil.

The other type of sucking or chewing is called wool-sucking. This occurs most often in Siamese or part-Siamese cats. These cats seem to have a strong attraction to the lanolin in wool or to human sweat on clothing. The behavior tends to start when the kitten is about four months or older. It begins with sucking on wool or other cloth and may progress to chewing or eating those and other materials. If you are lucky the cat will grow out of the problem, but some don't.

Try using taste aversion to stop the habit. Hide all your good clothing. Leave out a few old sweaters that you have sprayed with perfume and Bitter Apple spray or hot pepper oil. Your cat will learn to associate the smell of your perfume with the bad taste. Then you can apply perfume to your good sweaters to keep the cat away. Eventually you may be able to leave out all wool items safely.

Another approach is to increase the amount of fiber in the cat's diet. One theory is that the cat sucks on wool because of a desire for more fiber. Ask your veterinarian about this approach. You may either add fiber to the diet (using bran cereal or psyllium [Metamucil]) or feed a high-fiber diet (a "diet" cat food). Sometimes it helps simply to feed dry food instead of canned.

Consider providing a plant for your cat to chew. Grow catnip or grass in a flat dish. Rotate among several dishes as one gets "grazed down." Also look for dog chew toys for your cat. Get chew toys with a soft texture.

Often the habit is so ingrained that you have to manage it rather than eliminate it altogether. Some people train their cats to suck on just one item, such as an old sweater, and to leave other things alone.

CHILDREN AND CATS

Are your children ready for a cat? Is your cat ready for your new baby? No matter who came first, it's important that they live in harmony.

Children and cats get along famously as long as their personalities are matched. Choose a kitten that is outgoing and calm. Then teach your children how to care for and play with the cat. Show them how to pick up and hold a cat properly, supporting the front end with one arm and the rear legs with the other. Ask young children to sit down before they hold the cat.

Children must learn how to play with a cat correctly, both for the cat's comfort and their own safety. That way everyone has fun and no one gets scratched or bitten. Establish household "kitty-play" rules and stick by them. Teasing is off-limits, as is tail-pulling. Although it may seem harmless at first, using hands, arms, or feet for wrestling or playing with a cat should not be allowed. Cats don't know when play stops and pain begins, and they may inflict painful bites or scratches.

To avoid problems, play with cats using toys only, and never use your hands. Tie a cat toy to a string so your children can play safely with the kitten. Watch the kitten for signs of tiring, and be sure your children let her have time to herself.

What about a new baby in the house? How will your cat adjust to the child? Will it be safe to leave the two together?

Your cat may experience a bit of anxiety after you bring a new baby home. You used to pay lots of attention to kitty, and now your mind is occupied elsewhere. Be sure to set aside a few minutes each day to reassure your cat that you still love her.

A cat that seems jealous is most likely upset about the change in routine. (See "Emotions.") You can help your cat adjust to a new baby by making changes ahead of time. For instance, will your cat be kept out of baby's room while baby is sleeping? Then train kitty to stay out of that room well before the baby comes home. Consider installing a screen door that will allow you to hear the baby but keep the cat out.

Make changes in your schedule gradually when possible. Encourage kitty to be more independent during the months before your child's birth. You can even get a tape-recording or video of babies crying to acquaint your cat with the sound.

Although most cats are probably fine around babies, it's best not to leave the two alone and unattended. Small children don't know that they can't pull the cat's tail, and the cat doesn't know that the child can't look out for himself.

CLAWS, CLIPPING

Clipping your cat's claws doesn't have to be a dreaded chore. You can train kitty to sit still while her claws are trimmed. The process isn't painful, and if your cat is reasonably pleasant, you are perfectly capable of doing it yourself. But if your cat resists too much, you can always ask your groomer or the vet to do it for you.

First you need to know the cat's toe anatomy. Then you need to be sure that you have the proper tools for the job.

Your cat's feet have a similar structure to your own hands and feet, with a few modifications made by nature. The front feet each have five *digits,* which we usually call toes. There are four toes on the back feet. Some cats have six or seven toes—a sign of good luck.

The first digit, or dewclaw, is higher up on the inside of the front leg. The dewclaw corresponds to our thumb. In cats it doesn't serve much use. Dewclaws are always present on the

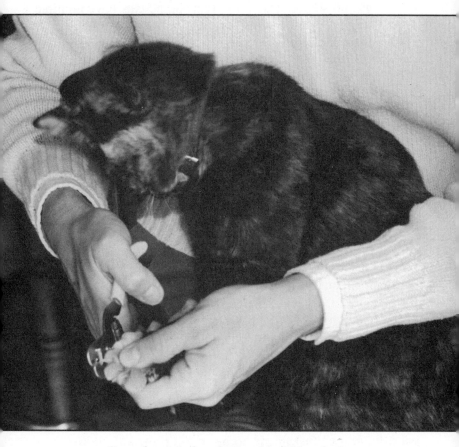

Keep the cat's leg close to his or her body when clipping claws.

front legs and sometimes on the rear. Some cats have multiple dewclaws.

The distal phalanx (toe bone) is partially contained within the cat's claw. Near the top of the bone is the area of specialized cells from which the claw grows. The cells die and form a hard layer of horny tissue that is pushed out by the cells behind. The rate of growth depends on many factors, but mostly on your cat's general health.

When should you trim your cat's claws? Some cats never need a trim. They do a fine job of wearing down their own claws. Kittens' claws need to be trimmed often to prevent "playful" trauma to your skin or furniture.

An older, sedentary cat will need frequent trims since the claws aren't worn as fast. Check the claws once a month to be sure they aren't growing too long. The claw should arch outward and should not begin to curl back toward the foot.

Be sure that you have the appropriate clippers or trimmers for your job. Cat claw trimmers come in several varieties and are available at grocery and pet stores. A pair of ordinary fingernail clippers will do for clipping a small cat's claws. The clippers should be sharp and rust-free.

Start by being sure your cat will let you touch and manipulate her paws without fuss. Don't even pick up the trimmers at first. With kitty sitting in your lap, pick up a paw and hold it across the four fingers of your open palm. Press kitty's toes between your thumb and first finger, so her claws protrude. Be sure you can do this without the clippers in your hand before you try to clip the claws.

Watch kitty's body while you hold her foot. Many times a cat will struggle. This is not because she doesn't want her feet handled, but because you are pulling her leg out at an uncomfortable angle or are holding her up in the air when she wants to feel something solid under her feet. When you grasp each foot for trimming, extend it only as much as is necessary to be able to extrude the claw. You can reach each claw easily without pulling the entire leg up and away from kitty's body.

If kitty resists this simple handling, work on that until she relaxes. Forget about trimming the claws for now. You don't have to get the claws clipped this week. If you create a fight, kitty will definitely not let you clip her claws next time. Do your paw-touching exercise any time that kitty is sitting on your lap purring. Don't bother kitty when she's excited and ready to play.

Each time, pet the toes, then pick up and massage the foot. Push down on each claw to extend it away from the digit. Give your cat lots of praise. Try to stop the exercise *before* she becomes irritated or draws away. Repeat daily until you can handle all four feet with no fuss.

Once your cat accepts being handled, then clipping the claws is easy. Set your clippers near your easy chair and wait for kitty to jump up for petting. Push out the claws of one foot with one hand, and use your clippers to snip off the sharp tip of each claw. If kitty pulls back, don't resist. Let her pull back, then gently grasp the foot again and continue. The minute you suspect that your cat is not having fun, stop. To keep the experience positive, you should stop *before* kitty loses her patience. (If you wait to stop until she raises a fuss, she will learn that her resistance makes you stop.)

How much can you trim off? Look at the claws of a white cat to get a good idea of where you should clip. Cats with white toes have an easily visible "quick," the pink area of blood vessels within the claw. Viewed from the side, the area you want to avoid forms a triangular shape. The excess claw curves down and away from that triangle.

The pink quick (live tissue) is within the triangle. The clear part of the claw that curves down and away is dead claw.

Keep a styptic pencil nearby in case you nick the quick. And when you do so, don't berate yourself. Anyone who has trimmed very many cat claws has nicked one occasionally. Hold a tissue to the claw, then apply a styptic pencil. You also can use styptic powder applied with a moistened cotton-tipped swab.

Apply ice if you don't have a styptic pencil, then hold a clean tissue to the claw for several minutes until bleeding stops.

Remember: (1) The bleeding *will* stop, sometimes even if you do nothing; (2) While your cat felt a little pinch, the pain does not last; (3) Chances of infection are minuscule; (4) *Everyone* who has trimmed an animal's claws has drawn blood once in a while; and (5) Bloodstains are easily removed with hydrogen peroxide.

COLLARS AND IDENTIFICATION

Does your cat wear a collar? Have you avoided using one for fear he could become hurt from its use? Or do you assume that your indoor cat doesn't need a collar?

A collar is safe and is necessary for all cats—especially those that never go outdoors. It only takes one accident for your cat to slip out and wander off. If kitty were ever injured, how would you be contacted?

Let's say you are planning a weeklong trip across country to your new home. Your cat, Blackie, will ride in the car in his carrier. He's never had a collar before, and you wonder whether he needs one now.

An identification collar is essential for traveling cats. No matter how careful you are, mistakes do happen. A collar is an inexpensive piece of insurance that you won't lose your cat forever.

What kind of collar is best? Many types of safety collars are available for cats. Some use elastic while others use Velcro. No matter what is used, the result is that the collar will release or stretch if it becomes caught on something. Use a harness instead of a neck collar for walking your cat on a leash. (For information on flea collars, see "Fleas.")

Use a brightly colored collar so your cat is easily visible. But don't rely on a reflective collar to prevent your cat from being run over by a car; keeping kitty indoors is the only way to do that.

Be sure to apply the collar snugly. If you can slip the collar over your cat's head, it is too loose. Many people leave collars loose in a mistaken attempt to keep their cats comfortable. Sometimes the cat reaches up with a paw and the paw becomes caught between the collar and the neck. As the cat struggles, the leg works its way through so the collar ends up around the cat's armpit.

The collar should not be too tight either. You should just be able to slide two fingers under it. Check the fit frequently on kittens since they grow faster than you might think.

The first time you apply a collar, your cat may try to scratch it off. As soon as you put the collar on, feed or play with your cat to temporarily distract him. Then let him alone and don't fuss over his discomfort. He will adjust quickly.

Get a name tag to attach to the collar. You can buy tags at any veterinarian's office or pet store. Or you may decide to use an engraver to write your name and phone number on the back of kitty's rabies tag. Consider adding a friend's phone number also, in case kitty is lost while you are traveling and not at home to receive calls.

What about a leash? Most cats can be trained to walk on a leash. If you are going to travel for more than a couple of days with your cat, he will be much happier if he can go for walks. (See "Leash Training" for details.)

DEAFNESS

Kittens are born deaf. Their hearing gradually develops over the next few months. Cats can hear all the sound frequencies that you can, plus higher frequencies you may miss. Cats use their acute hearing to locate prey during nighttime hunting.

Some cats are partially or completely deaf. Deafness can be due to age, injury, infection, or congenital abnormality.

Many, but not all, blue-eyed white cats are deaf. In white cats with one blue eye, deafness is found about twice as often as it is in ordinary cats. In white cats with two blue eyes, deafness is found from three to five times more often than in ordinary cats.

Whether a cat has one or two blue eyes doesn't correlate with whether he is deaf in one or both ears. Sometimes only one ear is affected, but often both ears are deaf. White cats with long hair are more likely to be deaf in both ears than white cats with short hair.

Deafness in just one ear may go unnoticed, with the cat's behavior attributed to stubbornness or stupidity. A deaf cat should never be allowed outdoors since he cannot hear danger approaching.

You can learn to communicate with your deaf cat. Sometimes the cat can hear a loud clap or a certain pitch of your voice better than a normal voice. Another option is to carry soft toys to throw near your cat when you want to get his attention.

You can wave your hand to call your cat or stomp your feet to get his attention. You might use one stomp to call your cat and three stomps to announce dinner. Some people teach their cats specific hand signals for "come" and other commands. First they stomp their feet to get the cat's attention, then they give the hand signal. (See "Training: Come, Sit, or Fetch.")

DECLAWING PROS AND CONS

Are you thinking of declawing your cat? Perhaps the cat has scratched your children or your furniture once too often.

Declawing is a controversial procedure. It is temporarily painful and is not strictly necessary. Therefore, you should try other means of training your cat before resorting to this surgery. It *is* possible to train your cat not to scratch the furniture. (See "Scratching Furniture.") Declawing is not a solution for cats that scratch people since they may simply resort to biting. It is best to train the cat not to be aggressive with people at all. (See "Biting, Scratching, and Clawing People.")

One alternative to declawing is to use commercially made plastic claw covers that are glued onto the nails to cover the sharp tips. Available through veterinarians, these claw covers must be reapplied periodically. This could be a short-term solution while you train your cat not to scratch, or it could be a long-term, permanent solution for certain cats. Keeping the claws trimmed short also minimizes damage.

Some cats have such bad scratching behavior that only declawing will allow them to continue to live with their owners. If yours is one, then declawing may be your best choice. Declawing is usually done on the front feet only. The operation is simpler and less painful on kittens than it is on older cats. A kitten's claws are smaller, have less tendency to bleed, and will heal faster than an older cat's. Older cats may take a few months to adjust to their new lack of claws.

Research has shown that there are no long-term behavior problems associated with declawing cats at any age. The majority of owners of declawed cats are satisfied with their cats' attitude and behavior after declawing.

The declawing operation removes the claw and the bed of tissue from which it originates. Some veterinarians use surgical glue to bring the skin edges together, while others may place a small, absorbable stitch. Bandages are usually applied overnight to prevent any bleeding. The operation often is done at the same time the cat is altered.

Expect your cat to be a little sore after the operation. You will need to replace the regular cat litter with shredded newspaper so the granules don't irritate the paws.

Occasionally a few spots of blood are seen during the day or two after the surgery. This is not cause for alarm. If you see more blood than that, or if your cat seems especially sore after several days, then you should call your veterinarian.

The declawing operation has very few complications. The short-term pain is easily managed with pain-relieving drugs administered by your veterinarian.

Some cats become overzealous in licking their paws after surgery. This reopens the wounds, slows healing, and predisposes the area to infection. While it's normal for cats to lick their paws, excessive licking does *not* clean the area or help it in any way. It may be a clue that your cat's paws are not healing normally.

Declawed cats can still hunt and climb trees. They still use their scratching posts (remember, the scratching motion does more than sharpen claws), and they can still ascend their indoor cat trees. But cats that are declawed should not be allowed outdoors, since they may not defend themselves or climb trees as well as before. However, there are no studies that show that declawed cats have any increased risk of injury.

If you are considering having your cat declawed, discuss the issue with your veterinarian to be sure you are comfortable with your decision.

DEFECATING OUT OF THE LITTER BOX

The complaint of defecating outside the box is less common than urinating outside the box. However, several of the same precautions apply to both urination and defecation problems. Start by reading "Urinating Outside the Box" and "Litter Box Training and Type of Litter."

Is kitty's box kept clean? Some cats refuse to use their box when it is full and dirty. You should remove feces daily and clean the entire box at least weekly.

Do you have several cats? Perhaps you need to provide more boxes than you now have. Is the box in a quiet place? Are you using litter that your cat likes?

Sometimes a dirty litter box or disliked litter starts the bad behavior, but the cat continues to use a new area after it becomes a habit. In that case you must retrain your cat to use the box.

The next item to check is kitty's stool. Cats with diarrhea get the urge to defecate so often that they may not make it to the box. A cat that is mildly constipated also may stop using her box. Take your cat plus a fresh stool sample to the veterinarian's office for an exam to confirm and treat these problems.

Sometimes cats will defecate on a bed when their owners are absent for several days. People usually attribute this action to the cat's anger at being left alone. It is more likely that the cat feels separation anxiety. Another possibility is that the litter box is being cleaned less than normal.

Be sure your cat-sitter removes feces from the box daily. Close the bedroom door while you are away. Ask the sitter to play with your cat every day to ease her loneliness.

DEPRESSION, BOREDOM, AND LONELINESS

Do you worry that your cat is lonely or bored while you are away at work? Is your cat an indoor cat with no playmates? Does your cat become destructive when you leave?

Your cat may suffer from separation anxiety if you leave for several days. Signs of separation anxiety include urinating or defecating outside of the litter box (especially on your bed); uprooting plants; or otherwise making a mess. To prevent future problems, close off certain rooms in your house and cat-proof the rest. (Put plants out of reach and so on.) Get a cat-sitter who can play with your cat every day.

Is your cat lonely? Two cats are often better than one. Consider getting a second cat as a playmate for the first. Read the guidelines about adopting a kitten that will get along with your cat. (See "Adopting Your Special Cat" and "Introducing Cats.")

If you can't get a second cat, don't feel as if you are depriving your cat of needed companionship. Cats are equally content to be alone or with others. The cat that lives in solitude simply needs other types of diversion and entertainment to keep her from becoming bored.

Your cat can have fun when you are away. Be creative in thinking of ways to keep her entertained. Rotate toys occasionally for variety. Tie a toy to a rope and suspend it from a chair. Leave an empty paper bag on the floor.

Get several soft balls for your cat. Rub catnip on the scratching post for a surprise that kitty will find when she walks by.

Cats like to look outside. Clear out a place where your cat can sit near a window. Most houses naturally have such a spot, but if yours doesn't, make a window ledge for your cat. Open a window to allow fresh air inside. Be sure the screen is fastened securely.

Leave the radio on to a station playing music your cat enjoys.

Cats need entertainment while you are away.
(Photo courtesy of Cat House Originals)

If you don't know what music your cat likes, try playing different stations while you are home and watching your cat's reaction. Some cats like to watch TV. If yours does, leave the TV on or play a videotape showing birds or fish.

Consider giving kitty a cat tree or cat house. Chances are that you have seen some of the fancy cat trees that are sold for cats. They are all some combination of boxes, platforms, and scratching surfaces. Cat trees and cat houses come in all shapes and sizes.

A simple cat tree might be a carpet-covered box with one ledge above it. Some are made with little tree houses that the cat can crawl into and hide. More elaborate models have several tiers with more than one house. Some extend all the way to the ceiling.

If you can't afford to buy a cat tree, you can make one yourself. Get carpet remnants from a local store and nail them firmly onto your frame. Be sure the tree is sturdy enough to withstand a cat swinging on it from above. The base should be wide enough to prevent tipping.

A cat tree will satisfy your cat's need to climb and scratch. It provides a high perch from which kitty can look down and feel safe. Cats like to be up high and to hide in small closed areas. A tree house provides a way to satisfy both these needs.

Just about any cat can learn to play on a cat tree, even if the cat has not seen one before. Declawed cats don't have any difficulty climbing up. Rub a little catnip on the tree to get kitty interested. Pull one of kitty's toys on a string, up and over the top of the tree. Soon your cat will realize that this huge toy is all for her—what a treat!

Sometimes a cat will become lonely and depressed when a close companion dies. The loss of one cat can be as hard on the other cat as it is on you. The remaining cat may stop eating, stop playing, and mope around. You need to provide extra attention and have patience. You and your cat can comfort each other. Eventually, perhaps, you may be ready for another addition to your home.

Whether your cat is lonely, depressed, or bored, you can bring more pleasure into her life. A consistent schedule and quality time mean a lot to your cat. Make the most of the times you are at home by playing with your cat, talking to her, and giving her lots of attention. Greet her the minute you come in the door after work. Chat with her while you make dinner. Gather her on your lap while you watch the news on TV.

Cats love routine, and they become accustomed to your work schedule. Your cat will learn that she gets plenty of loving during the times that you *are* at home.

DISCIPLINE AND DISOBEDIENCE

Every cat owner has discovered that you can't make a cat do anything she doesn't want to do. Using positive reinforcement works better to convince kitty to do what you want.

Yet punishment or negative reinforcement is sometimes necessary too. Use punishment when teaching kitty not to get into the garbage, not to jump on the kitchen counter, or not to eat your plants. When we say "punishment," we mean using a negative experience, distraction, or surprise to stop kitty from doing something.

Every cat can learn a signal that tells her to stop what she is doing. There is no bad behavior that you must "learn to live with." Training your cat is necessary for her own safety too. Think of your cat as a small child: You wouldn't let a child crawl on the kitchen counter or chew on plants, would you? Of course not—you would be concerned about the child's safety. Your cat *can* be trained. All you have to do is *consistently insist* on good behavior.

All household members must agree on the "kitty rules" before you begin. Decide what kitty is allowed to do, what is off-limits, and what discipline will be used.

Hitting or spanking a cat isn't necessary and usually won't work. Cats respond to force by either fighting back or running away. Also, rarely can you actually get your hands on your cat when she is bad. Using devices from afar is easier for you and gets better results.

Discipline alone doesn't always work with cats. To be able to stop some problems, you must find out why your cat is misbehaving. It may be necessary to provide your cat with an alternative behavior in addition to telling her no. (See "Training Basics" for the reasons behind your cat's disobedience.) For instance, you cannot get your cat to stop scratching the furniture unless you give her a scratching post.

One good way to get your cat to stop doing something is to spray her with water. A water bottle with a squirt top works better than toy squirt guns, which tend to leak. Set the sprayer to a setting that ejects a thin stream over a long distance rather than a fine spray that won't travel far.

Make the water blast fast and sharp so kitty doesn't think this is a new game. Some cats, though, don't seem to mind getting wet. For those cats, try loud noises.

Make a distraction device by putting a few pennies or stones into a tin can and closing the top. Shake the can loudly when kitty jumps on the table. Make a loud smack by slapping a ruler against a magazine. Use a party horn, a bicycle horn, or a loud whistle for noise. Louder horns may be purchased at electronic stores. Another simple way to make a loud noise is to clap your hands and hiss.

Sometimes cats don't respond to the noise you make. These cats are not sufficiently frightened by the noise to prevent them from repeating whatever they were doing. Try using a louder horn and be sure you act immediately when such a cat misbehaves.

On the other hand, if your cat seems excessively frightened by the noise, you may need to tone it down a bit. Use your cat's response to find out what is necessary to get her to stop her bad behavior but not become too scared. Every cat is different.

You should carry your device with you or keep it in easy reach. It's a good idea to leave at least one device in every room.

Whether you use a water bottle or a noisemaker, it must be used *at the very instant* that your cat begins to misbehave. That way the behavior itself is associated with a loud noise or blast of water. Use your device only long enough to make your cat stop her action. The noise or blast of water should be brief and sudden to startle your cat.

After you have made your cat stop the bad behavior, you should go about your business as usual. Don't try to approach the cat and apologize, or you will confuse her. Cats should be disciplined in a calm, matter-of-fact manner.

For instance, watch for the instant when kitty is just beginning to launch herself into the air to jump on the table. Try to squirt her in midair or sound the loud noise *as she jumps.* Of course, if you have just entered the room, you can make your move when kitty is already on the table.

But you can't punish kitty after the fact. Using your device even a few seconds after your cat has been bad is not going to work. If your cat tipped over your glass of juice while you were out of the room, it doesn't do any good to yell at her when you discover the mess five minutes later. She's already thinking of something else.

A cat cannot understand the consequences of her actions. If you come home and find the garbage can overturned, you cannot show that to your cat, give her a spanking, and expect her to understand. All she knows is that you came home and spanked her.

Your cat may learn to hide when you come home and the garbage can is overturned, but she doesn't know that she is being punished for the act of overturning the can. Her "guilty look" is because she knows that when there is a mess on the floor, you get mad.

Your cat will learn the fastest if she is *never* allowed to complete a bad behavior. You have to catch her in the act every time. If kitty occasionally is allowed to get away with bad behavior (such as when you are in another room or aren't home), you will have a much harder time training her. That means that you must supervise your cat or confine her to keep her out of trouble.

Set aside one room with your cat's food, water, toys, and litter box. Confine kitty there when you are not home or can't watch her. This is not "punishment," since your cat will come to think of her room as a safe place. Visit your cat for play and petting if she has to be confined for very long. Once your cat is trained, you can let her roam the entire house.

Set "booby traps" to punish your cat for certain behaviors in your absence. Booby traps should surprise but not hurt the cat. For example, set a pile of empty soda cans on the kitchen counter so they easily fall when kitty jumps up. An empty soda can set on the toilet paper roll will scare kitty when she tries to unroll the paper. Booby traps are practical and effective because the cat doesn't associate the punishment with you.

DISCIPLINE TOOLS

Use of the following training tools is described in detail in the sections discussing specific behavior problems. These lists are for your convenience.

Training tools include deterrents like this planter top.
(Photo courtesy of Kelstar)

Use to Make Kitty Stop Doing Something

- Spray water bottle
- Tin can with a few pebbles or coins inside (shake for noise)
- *Loud* horn (bicycle horn, warning horn, whistle)
- Hair dryer (placed near the place kitty misbehaves, with a remote switch)
- Remote-controlled whistle or motion detector with alarm (obtain at stores such as Radio Shack)
- Soft toys (throw when kitty is playing with something he shouldn't be)

Use on Objects or in Areas You Want Kitty to Avoid

- Double-sided tape
- Mousetraps (set upside down, or under sheets of foil, or with the catch wire bent so it can't trap the paw)
- Pyramid of empty soda cans
- Foil or plastic wrap
- Note: *Do not* use mothballs. They are toxic to cats and your cat could become poisoned by chewing on one.

Use on Objects That Kitty Chews or Eats

- Bitter Apple spray
- Hot sauce or hot pepper oil
- Mustard
- Cayenne pepper mixed with oil or water
- Floral- or citrus-scented room deodorizer spray
- Strongly scented deodorant spray

DROOLING

You are petting your cat in his favorite spot when you notice your hand is all wet. Kitty is drooling all over you! Is this normal?

Some cats drool when they are extremely content. They may drool and knead while you pet or scratch them. In these cases, there is no cause for alarm. Unfortunately, there is also not much you can do about the problem. You can stop petting at the point when your cat begins to drool. Keep a towel by the couch for the times when you pet your cat a lot.

A cat that drools at other times is likely to have a problem in his mouth. Open your cat's mouth to take a look. Use one hand to hold the upper jaw while the other hand opens the lower jaw. If your cat reaches up with his front paws, wrap him tightly in a towel.

Examine the tongue and throat for redness, lumps, or sores. Lift the side of kitty's lip and look at the outside edges of the teeth. Be sure to look at the teeth that are far back in the mouth, since these are usually affected most. Is there a lot of tartar buildup? (If you can see any, it is a lot. Imagine what your dentist would say if your teeth looked like that!) Look at the gum line where the teeth meet the gums. Is it red or swollen?

Whether you see anything or not, your cat still should be examined by a veterinarian. Looking in your cat's mouth just helps you get a better idea of what is going on. If the teeth are brown or black, or the gums are very red, you can tell the vet your cat may need his teeth cleaned.

EMOTIONS: AFFECTION, JEALOUSY, ANGER, AND ESP

Cats have gotten a bad rap for decades. "They never make good pets because they are so independent," some say. Others proclaim, "A cat will never become attached to you the way a dog will."

Nonsense. A cat can be just as loving, dependent, and attached to you as you like. Cats are affectionate and responsive. Every cat's behavior is a result of how he is treated. If you ignore your cat, he will ignore you. If you talk to him, pet him, and play with him often, he will be attached to you.

Cats certainly can take care of themselves when necessary. They don't need the same kind of care as a dog. But cats also dearly love your companionship. Your cat will be just as aloof or as friendly as you expect him to be.

Most cat owners think of their cats as close companions or members of the family. People talk to their cats, sleep with their cats, and celebrate their cats' birthdays. Cats greet their owners at the door, follow them about, and come when called. They affectionately rub against and knead on people when they are content.

What if your cat doesn't seem as friendly as you would like him to be? Start paying more attention to kitty. Call his name when you come in the door and when you feed him. Get some toys and play with your cat. Talk to kitty every time you see him.

Do cats experience anger, jealousy, or loneliness? Imagine you have just returned from a weekend vacation. You left plenty of food and water for your cat and had a neighbor check in on him. You open the door and find your house a mess. The plants have been uprooted and kitty has pooped on the bed. Of course, you assume, the cat did all this to retaliate against your leaving.

Scientists insist that animals don't have the same feelings as people do. Yet you know that your cat's actions cannot all be explained by instinct and a desire for food and water. We will never know exactly what our cats feel, but we can make a good guess after we study feline behavior.

Be careful not to assume a motivation on your cat's part that may not exist. Your cat's priorities differ from yours, so the reasons for his behavior do too.

Perhaps your cat urinates on your bed or your favorite chair when you are away for several days. Although you may think your cat did so out of spite, it is more likely that he felt separation anxiety. The cat was attracted to a place where your scent was strongest.

Getting into plants and otherwise making a mess while you are gone could be your cat's way of relieving boredom. It also could be another way of relieving separation anxiety.

The best approach to these problems is to "cat-proof" your house before you leave. Close the bedroom door and cover the planters with foil or plastic wrap to keep kitty out of the dirt. Leave lots of toys out. Ask your cat-sitter to play with your cat while you are away. (For more tips, see "Depression, Boredom, and Loneliness.")

Do cats feel jealousy? Perhaps you have gotten a new kitten and your older cat suddenly begins to misbehave. Or you just had a baby and kitty seems out of sorts. Although it is easy to ascribe the cat's attitude to jealousy, another cause is more likely. Cats become stressed when any change in routine occurs. It is likely the cat's eating, play, and sleeping schedules have been altered. You may show a different attitude toward your cat now than you did before.

The best cure for "jealousy" is to return to a consistent schedule as soon as possible. Set aside time each day to play with your cat. Even if you have less time available, your cat will appreciate a regular play time.

Make changes ahead of time if you anticipate a disruption in your lifestyle. For instance, if you are expecting a baby, you might not want the cat in the same room where the baby sleeps.

Start training your cat to stay out of that room now. If a different person will feed the cat after the baby is born, have that person start now.

Approach other potential causes of jealousy the same way. Consider the changes that will occur and try to make them gradually. (See "Introducing Cats" for more suggestions.)

Can cats be embarrassed? Perhaps you have seen your cat accidentally fall off somewhere he was casually lying. After the fall, he sits up, looks around, and quickly begins to groom himself. Cats often groom themselves when they feel a bit uncomfortable or "embarrassed."

Although cats are said to be solitary animals, they do form bonds with each other. When two cats become close and one is lost or dies, the remaining cat may be depressed for months. A depressed cat may meow constantly or stop eating. Lots of loving and comfort is needed in these cases.

Cats are emotional creatures. Cats may feel lonely, bored, frightened, and stressed. They show stress in a variety of ways, from overgrooming to forgetting their toilet habits. Many behavior problems are caused by the cat's sensitive nature. To change behavior problems, you must understand their cause. (See "Depression, Boredom, and Loneliness" and "Training Basics.")

Do cats have ESP? Cats have been credited with predicting earthquakes or hurricanes. Reports exist of cats becoming excited, restless, or fearful before an earthquake, even when sensitive instruments don't pick up any problem. The cat may detect variations in electromagnetic fields, air pressure, the earth's level, gases in the air, or some other changes that we can only imagine.

Cats use their whiskers to detect minor changes in air vibrations and currents. Perhaps this explains their seeming ability to predict hurricanes. Changes in the barometric pressure also may affect cats.

Some cats have an innate sense of "homing behavior" that doesn't require remembering a certain route. Certain cats have been known to return home after being lost miles away. Other cats go back to their old home after their owners have moved. Cats may take a more direct route to their destination than the way they left. Not all cats do this, so don't rely on your cat's homing behavior to get him back when he's lost.

Since we don't know exactly what the cat is sensing when he seems to predict an earthquake or find a home from far away, it's hard to say whether the cat has "ESP" or not. But if extrasensory perception simply means that the cat senses something we do not, then we can say with certainty that is true.

EYESIGHT AND BLINDNESS

Do cats have better eyesight than people? "Different" is a more apt description than better or worse. Kittens open their eyes at one to two weeks of age. The cat's eyesight gradually matures over the next few months. Cats are slightly nearsighted and don't see objects as sharply as you do.

Do cats see color? Cats do have the "cone" cells in the retina that perceive color, but they have fewer cone cells than people do. Your cat probably sees colors as a bit more washed out than you see them. Colors in the cat's view may contain more gray tones than the colors you see.

Yet cats can see differences in brightness that you would never detect. Cats are also much better at following moving objects than are dogs. Just compare a cat and a dog watching an insect in the air.

You probably have noticed that your cat sees better in the dark than you do. The cat's eye is specially adapted for night vision. A reflective area in the back of the eye reflects the available light to aid night vision. That's what causes the glow you see when you shine a light into a cat's eyes at night.

Cats may be born with vision deficits. Blue-eyed white cats sometimes lack the reflective area in the back of the eye. These cats don't see as well at night as other cats.

You may notice that some Siamese cats appear "cross-eyed." Eyes of Siamese cats are anatomically different from those of other cats. The two eyes don't connect normally to the brain. Siamese cats don't have binocular vision and thus have impaired depth perception.

Every Siamese cat is affected, but the degree of abnormality varies from cat to cat. The syndrome is connected genetically to the Siamese coat color and pattern. The same syndrome occurs in albino cats and in some Burmese and Himalayan cats. In most cases there is not a noticeable problem with the cat's vision.

Some cats are blind. Blind cats can do well as pets but they must be kept indoors. They will learn their way around the house and will fare well as long as you don't change the furniture around.

Blindness may be congenital or it may be acquired due to injury or disease. It is important to have your veterinarian examine your cat if you notice vision problems. While a blind cat may appear comfortable, he may be suffering from some treatable discomfort due to the eye disease. Your veterinarian can help determine whether any treatment is necessary.

FEEDING CHANGES AND NEW DIETS

Is your cat on a weight-loss program? Perhaps kitty has an illness that requires a therapeutic diet. No matter what the reason, a change in diet can be difficult.

Your cat may refuse to eat the new food at first. You may be tempted to return to the old food. It is worthwhile to make the switch, though, since kitty's health will benefit and he is likely to live a longer, more comfortable life.

Change the diet gradually to help kitty adjust. On the first day, make a mixture of three fourths of his old food with one fourth of the new one. Continue feeding this mix until your cat eats his usual amount without hesitation. (It may take a week or more.)

Then mix the new and old foods fifty-fifty. Continue feeding this mix, again, until kitty accepts it as normal. Then make a mix that is one fourth old food and three fourths new food, continuing until kitty adjusts. Finally you can feed only the new diet.

Don't feel as if you have to meet some kind of time schedule with each change. If your cat has a particularly difficult time adjusting, then consider adding something to flavor the food (clam juice, garlic, water from canned tuna; see "Appetite Loss"). However, do keep your goal in mind: eventually to feed only the prescribed food and nothing else. Mixing in other foods over the long term will defeat your purpose.

Cats that have trouble changing foods are sometimes those that always have been fed a very good-tasting diet free choice (food is always left out or is fed on demand). They have no reason to believe that their old diet won't appear again. One plan that may help is first to offer the old food in twice-daily feedings rather than on demand. This teaches the cat that food is not always available. Once the cat gets used to eating meals, then begin to slowly mix in the new food as just described.

While it is important to make the switch to the therapeutic

food, it's also important that your cat continues to eat. Cats, unlike people and dogs, cannot fast for very long without becoming ill. You must balance the need to change foods with the equally important need for your cat to eat. But if your cat won't eat the new food, don't just choose any good-tasting tidbit from the refrigerator to stimulate his appetite. Ask your vet about which foods are absolutely off-limits and which are acceptable.

For instance, a cat with kidney disease may not like his therapeutic diet. The cat loves tuna, though. Yet feeding too much protein could backfire and make the cat even sicker. A better choice is to flavor the new food with the water from a can of tuna. Eat the tuna yourself.

FEEDING FINICKY CATS

Charlie crouched in the corner looking guilty as I entered the kitchen. "What are you up to now?" I muttered, noticing the overturned garbage can. There wasn't much in there, since it had just been emptied the night before. What could he be after?

A quick look answered my question. Charlie had confiscated our cantaloupe rinds from that morning's breakfast. He'd already eaten a big chunk of the rind.

Since that morning many years ago, I've encountered many other cats with a love for cantaloupe. Does your cat like cantaloupe or have another taste preference?

Cats respond to the flavor, odor, shape, and texture of foods. Cat food must have a pleasant odor, since your cat carefully smells his food before eating. Some cats prefer soft food, while others prefer dry. The food's size must be easy to chew too.

Cats usually prefer fish and meat, and they often like dairy products, such as ice cream or yogurt. Although they have favorite flavors, most cats willingly eat any flavor of cat food. Taste tests show that cats can discern salty, sour, and bitter taste, but they don't have many tastebuds that recognize sweetness. Cats that appear to like sweets are likely responding to another flavor in the food.

A food's temperature also contributes to its appeal. The flavor of food is most apparent to a cat when the food is the same temperature as the cat's tongue.

Some cats like dog food and will raid the dog's dish. An occasional bite of dog food is not harmful to your cat, but if kitty eats more dog food than cat food he could become ill.

Your cat's nutritional needs are very different from your dog's. Cats need much more fat, protein, and B vitamins in their diets than dogs do. They also need an amino acid called taurine and will develop blindness or heart disease when it is deficient. Dog food doesn't contain enough taurine for cats. So keep your cat out of the dog's food bowl to keep him healthy.

You may wonder whether a cat's desire for a particular food reflects a need for a certain vitamin or other nutrient. That's not the case, though. Cats' preferences are based on flavor. Your cat shouldn't eat what he likes best all the time, any more than you should eat chocolate cake every day.

A cat's taste preferences are learned by the time he is six months old. You can help reduce the chances of your cat's becoming finicky by offering him a variety of foods and flavors when he is still a kitten.

Are cats really as finicky as their reputation portrays? When offered a variety of foods from kittenhood, cats will eat a variety as adults. Cats that are fed canned food may shun dry food, or the opposite may occur. Some cats eat better if they are stroked or talked to while they dine.

Cats eat less when they are disturbed, frightened, or in a strange place. (See "Appetite Loss" for tips.) A sick cat will become a finicky cat. Be sure to have your vet examine your cat if he won't eat.

Finicky cats train their owners to feed them certain foods. The cat learns that he can look at his food bowl and walk away. He knows that his owner then will get out something tastier to get him to eat. Is your cat training you that way?

Finicky cats don't take kindly to a change in diet, but you *can* change your cat's diet if necessary. Similarly, a cat that is accustomed to treats or table scraps also will protest if those are withheld. Yet healthy treats are available for cats on a diet.

You don't have to give in to every pleading look. Although cats shouldn't go without food for more than several days, they can wait to get hungry enough to eat what you offer instead of what they want. (See "Food Brands" for more tips.)

FEEDING MEALS VS. FREE CHOICE

Cats that live in the wild usually eat many small meals per day. That's the equivalent of your cat's free-choice feeding. But many healthy pets enjoy their twice-daily meals without a problem. Your cat will come to relish his meals either way, as long as his daily schedule is consistent.

The answer to the meals vs. free choice question depends on the type of food you offer and on your cat's weight. Dry food may be fed as meals, but it is usually offered free choice. Canned food cannot be left out so it must be fed as meals.

Cats that are prone to urinary disorders do best when offered food free choice. Eating small amounts all day causes the cat's urine to maintain a consistent pH (acidity), while eating meals causes undesirable wide swings in pH throughout the day.

How much should kitty eat? As long as your cat is healthy and not overweight, you can leave dry food out all the time and not worry about measuring an exact amount. As a general rule, the "average ten-pound cat" eats about one-half cup of food a day.

Many cats are overweight and must be fed measured amounts. Every cat food is made differently, so you cannot feed the same amounts of each interchangeably. Follow label instructions and ask your vet if you aren't sure. When feeding a measured amount, divide the total daily feeding into two or three meals.

FEEDING TREATS AND TABLE SCRAPS

There is nothing inherently wrong with table scraps. It's the *kind and amount* of scraps that determine whether the food is fit for kitty. Unfortunately, the parts of our meals that we usually give kitty are the worst for him—gristle, fat, gravy, and bones. And many people don't eat well themselves, so even the "good" parts of their meals aren't fit for their cats.

Since most people feed their cats some kind of treat no matter what their vet recommends, let's be honest and discuss the "better" treats versus the "absolutely off-limits" treats. Remember that even the acceptable treats will cause health problems if you feed too much. It doesn't matter if that one food is "healthy." For instance, giving your cat a lot of tuna or boiled egg is not good because that is not a balanced diet. Feed your cat mostly cat food, and keep the table scraps to a minimum. A *total* of one tablespoon of treats per day is best.

Offer different treats each time for variety. Keep the

amounts small. Your cat's food is complete and balanced, and you could upset that balance by feeding too much of one thing. For instance, feeding too much liver can cause vitamin A toxicity, so no more than one ounce of cooked liver should be offered to a grown cat per day. And feeding too many tasty treats results in a finicky, overweight cat with an annoying begging habit.

Acceptable "People Food" for Cats
(1 tablespoon maximum, per day)

Plain boiled meat	Boiled egg (1 Tbsp, *not* 1 egg)
Plain yogurt	
Air-popped popcorn (no salt/butter)	Canned tuna or clams
	Boiled vegetables
	Cooked liver

What about commercially available treats for cats? Use these in moderation too. They are no better or worse than table scraps. Don't let the label mislead you. Often the fat content is much higher than the minimum listed on the label. And a statement such as "100% nutritious" is meaningless. Limit these treats to one a day at most, or your cat may gain weight.

What about treats for an underweight cat? It is better to feed more of a balanced diet than to add one kind of food or give treats. (See "Weight Loss" for more tips.)

What kind of treats can you give an overweight cat? Avoid commercial treats, which can be very fattening. Instead, use part of your cat's normal food for treats. First measure out the total daily ration of canned or dry food for your cat. Then set aside a small portion for treats in between meals. Some cats like cooked vegetables or fruits. However, eating too much of these may cause gas or diarrhea.

What if someone else is sneaking treats to your cat? Sometimes a well-intentioned neighbor will slip your cat some food or goodies. Keeping your cat indoors is the only real solution.

You also can tape a short note on your cat's collar. Write "Please don't feed me, I'm a diabetic."

What about the cat that gets into the "people food" when you aren't looking? Here's where training becomes difficult. Even the most mannerly cat, when left alone in a room with a piece of fish on the counter, might give in to temptation.

One of the sacrifices you must make as a cat owner is that you can't just leave food out. When you are finished with dinner, put away those steak bones immediately so kitty doesn't get into them while you're relaxing in front of the TV.

On the other hand, some cats are so rude as to actually try to jump on the counter right in your presence. These cats have learned that nothing happens when they misbehave, so they don't have any qualms about jumping into the food. If your cat does this, you are being too nice and should go back and read the section on discipline. Negative reinforcement does not hurt your cat and helps her understand her boundaries.

Certain foods are off-limits for all cats. Foods that are too rich for any cat include processed meats (hot dogs and bacon), fried foods, most cheeses, and sweets. These foods contain too much salt, fat, or sugar for your cat.

Raw eggs, raw chicken, and raw turkey may contain *Salmonella* organisms, a cause of food poisoning. Feeding raw eggs also can cause a biotin deficiency. Other raw meats may contain bacteria or parasites that make kitty sick.

Off-limits Foods

Raw meat	Raw eggs
Raw fish	Bones
Processed meats	Fried foods
Milk	Junk food (chips, etc.)

Even though cats love milk, it is not good for them. Cats older than three months lose the ability to digest milk. Drinking milk will give most cats diarrhea.

Kittens should not receive cow's milk, since its nutrient balance is different from a cat's milk. If you have orphan kittens or if you are weaning a kitten onto solid food, you can purchase a cat milk replacer at your local pet store or veterinary clinic. Or just wet the kitten food with water to make it soft.

Fish is another trouble food. Eating raw fish causes a vitamin deficiency in cats. Raw fish contains an enzyme that destroys thiamine (vitamin B_1).

Cooked fish is not recommended as a large part of the diet either. Even after fish is cooked, it still could be low in vitamins B_1, A, and E. Feeding only fish could cause illness due to a vitamin deficiency.

Another concern with raw or cooked fish is that the fish can accumulate high levels of mercury or polychlorinated biphenyls. If you feed a lot of fish, these toxins could accumulate in your cat. Some veterinarians recommend not feeding fish-based cat food continually, but instead rotating these foods with other flavors.

An occasional treat of tuna or other cooked fish won't hurt your cat, though. Just keep the amounts in moderation.

Chocolate and onions are two foods that can be poisonous to cats. Your cat isn't likely to eat these foods. Avoid giving your cat a lot of chocolate milk or chocolate ice cream. (A little bit isn't likely to poison the cat, however.) Onion soup is one place where a cat might try to eat onions.

Bones or raw meat can make your cat sick. Yet cat owners frequently ask, "Why can't my cat eat raw meat or chicken bones? Don't cats naturally catch and eat birds and mice?"

Your offerings differ in many ways from that "wild" diet. Supermarket meat is not the same as a wild mouse. For instance, many raw meats can carry harmful bacteria that can cause food poisoning (far more often than a mouse would!).

The bones you may offer your cat also differ from its wild diet. Cooked bones become brittle and are more likely to break into slivers that could harm your cat.

Cats are carnivores, but that doesn't mean they eat only muscle meat. Wild carnivores eat the entire body of their prey, including the bones and intestinal contents. A cat fed only meat doesn't get a proper balance of nutrients and will suffer from rickets due to calcium deficiency.

On the other hand, cats can't survive on a vegetarian diet either. Cats must take in certain nutrients that are found only in meat, including taurine, arachidonic acid, and preformed vitamin A. (They can't use beta carotene, the precursor of vitamin A found in plants.) Also, the cat's urine must stay acidic to avoid urinary problems. A vegetarian diet creates alkaline (nonacidic) urine.

To keep your cat's diet balanced, feed mostly cat food. Use a commercially made food or ask your veterinarian for a recipe for a balanced diet you can make yourself.

FIGHTING CATS

Domino's owner was fed up. This was her third trip to the vet in three months. Another abscess, another surgery bill, and more antibiotics to give. "What can I do to make him stop fighting?" she asked. "He was neutered as a kitten. If only that bully cat from next door would leave him alone."

Fighting doesn't have just one solution, since the problem has so many different causes. Cats may fight with others in the same house or with neighborhood outdoor cats. Once you understand the reasons behind the fighting, you can stop it.

Domino was just doing what comes naturally to any cat. When another cat threatened his territory, he fought back. You can't blame the cats for this problem. It all comes back to you.

Domino's owner had already taken care of the first step in

preventing fights. It is essential that any cat with a fighting problem be altered as soon as possible, whether the cat is male or female. Remember, the cost of neutering is often less than the cost of surgical repair of an abscess. (An abscess is an infected bite wound that develops frequently in cats that fight.)

Male cats fight more often because testosterone affects portions of the brain that control aggressive behavior. Neutering males is 80 to 90 percent effective in stopping fighting, *no matter what the cat's age.*

In some cases there are an inordinate number of fights because of one or more stray cats in the neighborhood. (See "Stray Cats" for tips on reducing that problem.) But you can't get rid of all the cats that might wander into the neighborhood.

Other than neutering, the only other surefire prevention for fighting is to keep your cat indoors. After all, do you really expect all your neighbors to keep their cats inside just so yours can go out? It *is* possible for an outdoor cat to learn to live inside. (See "Outdoor Cats Converted to Indoor Cats" for tips.)

A different situation occurs when the fighting cats live in the same household. Altering both your male and female cats is the first step toward making peace. If you haven't done this, read no further, but call your vet for an appointment.

Cats fight for different reasons that have different solutions. Consider how and when the fighting started, and examine exactly what your cats do when a fight erupts.

Minor spats and occasional fights are to be expected when you add a new cat to your home, no matter how well adjusted the cats and how much space you have. Tip the odds in your favor by carefully choosing your new cat. (See "Introducing Cats.") Introduce a newcomer slowly by closing the cat in a separate room at first. Gradually allow the cats to have time together. Be patient. It may take months for the cats to adjust.

Some cats just don't get along with others. Cats that were weaned early and have grown up without being around other cats won't be social. They will either fight or become frightened and hide from other cats.

Another cause of fighting is overcrowding. Fighting can erupt in a multicat household after you add "just one more" cat. The problem is not the new cat, but that the total number of cats has reached a critical level that overcrowds all the cats. Fighting due to overcrowding is especially likely when there are more than five cats.

To ease the feeling of crowding, be sure every cat has his own bed and food dish. Provide lots of cat trees and cat houses so each cat has a place to hide or escape. Consider building an outdoor enclosure or run to further increase the cats' space.

Another cause of fighting is territorial defense. Does one cat bully another, chase him out of the room, and keep him in constant hiding? This kind of territorial aggression is hard to stop. Put cat trees and houses in several rooms to allow more space. Provide lots of positive attention to the bullied cat to build his self-confidence. Be sure he has at least a few hours each day when he is free from the bully. Give each cat the run of the house occasionally. Close one cat in a room by himself while the other cat has the run of the house, then switch their positions. You may need to make a permanent arrangement that gives each cat his or her own separate space in the home.

Chasing also can be a form of play with an aggressive cat (usually a kitten) continually pestering another cat (usually a shy, older cat). You can tell that this is not territorial aggression by watching the cat doing the chasing. Does he try to play with as well as chase the other cat? Does he hide and then pounce on the shy cat?

You can stop this play-attack by squirting the aggressor with water. Distract him with toys too. Use sponge balls or soft toys attached to strings. Throw a toy at the kitten when he is about to pounce. Use the string to drag the toy across the floor and tempt the kitten away from his original target. That gives him something to attack besides your other cat. Be persistent, since kitten energy is boundless. Eventually the kitten will grow up and relax.

Sometimes two cats that were friendly become hostile. A

problem may occur after one cat is hospitalized and then returns home. The cat's new odor makes him appear to be a stranger. If this happens, try slowly reintroducing the two as if you had just gotten a new cat.

Two previously friendly cats also may fight because of transferred aggression. For example, your cat sees a strange cat outside the window. The two exchange growls and hisses. Then your second cat approaches the first one, who lashes out in anger. This problem may recur if the strange cat makes a habit of strolling by your window. You will have to either get rid of the stray or block your cats' view of that area. If your cats continue to fight anyway, you should reintroduce them slowly.

No matter what you do, your cats may fight at times. When should you break up a cat fight? A little hissing or an occasional swat are nothing to be concerned about. Sometimes it is best to let the cats sort things out for themselves. But if one cat pins down another, if you hear lots of yowling, or if there is bloodshed, you must stop the fighting.

Stay at a distance or you will be hurt. You may trust your cat, but if he is angry and distracted, chances are he will strike out before he realizes it is you.

If you are outdoors, use a hose. Indoors, use a squirt bottle or make loud noises. If that doesn't work, you may have to dump a bucket of water on them. Be careful not to pick up a cat after he's been in a fight or he may take out his frustrations on you. Try to separate the cats by chasing one into a different room and closing the door. Or use a broom to shoo one cat away.

Sometimes two cats in a house won't stop fighting. You may have tried slowly introducing them, giving them separate spaces, and many other techniques. In these cases, you can get help from your vet. Two types of medications can reduce fighting: hormones and tranquilizers. Either may help to change the cat's attitude and aggression. Sometimes you may have to try a few medications until one is found that works.

Don't worry that drugs are bad or that your cat will have to take medicine forever. Consider the medication as an aid

Flea eggs and larvae accumulate where your cat sleeps.

to your training. Sometimes you must use both training and medication to make permanent changes. As the cats learn to live in harmony, you will reduce the dose of medicine gradually (usually over several months) until the cats behave normally without treatment. (Read "Introducing Cats" for more tips on reducing fights.)

FLEAS: CHEMICAL AND NATURAL CONTROL

Are fleas a continual problem in your home? Fleas can be controlled but not eliminated if your cat goes outdoors. An indoor cat stands a good chance of becoming flea-free. The flea control program for either cat is similar, but the outdoor cat needs repeated attention.

A cat that is allergic to flea bites develops a reaction from just one bite. The only way to relieve that cat's discomfort is to make her an indoor cat and to eliminate fleas altogether.

A lot of new information is being learned about fleas. You can control your flea problem better by understanding how fleas live. Adult fleas live their entire lives on the pet. Only the immature stages live off the animal. Fleas that you see in your home probably have just hatched, not jumped off your cat.

Fleas lay eggs on the cat. The eggs fall off and land on the bed, your carpet, and your furniture. Since the eggs are laid only on the cat, they drop off in highest numbers in places the cat spends most of her time. Most of them are found where your cat sleeps.

Eggs hatch into flea larvae within two weeks. Larvae turn into pupae, which then develop into adult fleas. The entire cycle from egg to adult takes from two months to a year. The cycle is fastest when it is warm and humid.

Over 90 percent of the fleas in your home are eggs and larvae. If you kill only adult fleas, you will never get them under control. Without doing something else, you are treating the end stage instead of tackling it at the beginning.

Flea larvae and eggs are resistant to many insecticides. Newer "insect growth regulators" (IGRs) kill eggs and prevent flea larvae from maturing. You can get house sprays, foggers, and cat sprays containing a combination of an IGR and an insecticide that kills the adults.

Simply dusting your cat with flea powder or putting on a flea collar will not control fleas. You must treat your cat, your home, and your yard for adult fleas, flea eggs, and flea larvae. The following program sounds like a lot of work, but if done properly, it will reduce the work you have in the future.

Schedule one day for "flea-free day," and treat your entire home for fleas. Start by washing all bedding (yours and the cat's). Dry it on the highest heat possible. Then mop, vacuum, dust, and clean the house. Throw the used vacuum bag in an outdoor, covered garbage can when you are finished. Remove all furniture cushions and set them next to the furniture. Clean the basement, garage, laundry room, and your car.

Once the house is clean, you can have it fogged or sprayed. You can do this yourself or hire an exterminator. Ask for products that will leave a residual effect in your home and yard. Use a product containing a combination of an IGR and an adulticide. Take all your pets elsewhere for the day.

You may find it convenient to have a groomer give your cat a flea shampoo or dip at this time. If not, the cat should get this treatment just before you fog the home. Then take the cat out of the house and do the fogging. That way you aren't bringing live fleas back when you return your cat to the treated house. Thoroughly air out your home before you bring the cat back.

All pets must be treated at the same time. If one pet has fleas, they all do—even if you can't see them. You can use shampoo, dip, spray, or powder. Follow the instructions on the label of the product you use. In general, dips should not be used more than once weekly, shampoos twice a week.

Sprays and powders can be used daily or several times a week. The best ones contain an IGR plus an insecticide to kill the adult fleas. (Pyrethrin is the safest.) Cats tolerate water-based products better than those with an alcohol base. Fluff up the hair to get the product to the skin. Be sure to cover the whole cat, but use a light mist or dusting. To get spray on the cat's head, spray a washcloth and then wipe the head.

The yard and porch must be treated too, if you have outdoor pets. Yard treatment doesn't have to be overwhelming. Very few fleas are found except where the pets lie or sleep a lot (the corner of the porch, for instance). After the yard is treated, do not allow your pets outside until the spray has dried.

It is important to understand the cumulative effects of the flea control products you use. Be careful not to poison your cat accidentally by exposing her to high doses of chemicals. For instance, don't put your just-dusted cat outdoors right after the yard has been sprayed. Don't put a flea collar on your cat the same day you spray, dust, shampoo, or dip.

The biggest problem occurs with organophosphate insecticides. If your home and yard are treated with an organophosphate, it is best to treat your cat with a different type of chemical. Your vet can tell you which products contain organophosphates.

Many flea control products made for dogs are not safe for cats, so be sure the label says "cats." Likewise, kittens are more susceptible than adult cats. Flea product labels will state the age at which the product is safe for kittens.

Outdoor cats should be dusted or sprayed with a flea control product several times a week. Repeat your house treatment throughout flea season as recommended on the product you use. A few immature fleas in your home will survive the first treatment. No products can kill the pupa stage of the flea. Repeat treatments eventually will kill these as they hatch.

If retreating your entire home seems too daunting, you can concentrate your efforts where the fleas accumulate. Remember that the adult fleas are on your pets. Most of the larvae and eggs are in areas where pets spend most of their time—their beds, a favorite windowsill, the top of the couch, or the carpet next to the sliding glass door.

Vacuum those favored areas every other day. Use an IGR spray in those spots at recommended intervals to prevent eggs and larvae from developing into adults. By doing so you will find that the number of fleas on your cat is dramatically reduced.

What about flea collars? At best, they keep the number of fleas down for a few weeks. Since you would have to use a spray or powder along with the collar anyway, you expose your cat to fewer chemicals by not bothering with the collar at all. One recommendation for use of a flea collar is to put it in your vacuum bag to kill fleas that you vacuum up. However, this could release toxic chemicals into the air.

Some people don't like to use too many chemicals, so they use only a little bit or they don't treat the cat and their entire premises at the same time. This strategy will backfire and leave them using even more chemicals, more often, because the fleas will never be under control. It is better to make a full attack early in the season to prevent the fleas from ever gaining a foothold.

To reduce the amount of insecticide you use, apply a desiccant product to your carpet for long-term flea control. These products kill fleas by drying them out. Use a product made for that purpose and carefully follow the instructions. Do not use Borax powder, which may harm your carpet and poison your cat. The desiccant will kill only the fleas that fall off the cat and those that hatch in the carpet, so you still have to treat the cat.

The best "low-chemical" approach is to vacuum every other day (including on and under furniture), wash all bedding once a week, and remove fleas from your cat with daily use of a flea comb. Use a desiccant on your carpet, an IGR fogger or spray in your home, and a combination IGR-adulticide spray on your cat. By using products that kill the immature fleas, you will end up with fewer fleas and less need for chemicals in the long run.

Scientific studies have shown that brewers' yeast, garlic, and ultrasonic collars do *not* control fleas. These products do not cause harm except that your cat continues to suffer from fleas if they are all you use. Plant-based products such as pyrethrum (from the chrysanthemum flower) are still insecticides and should be used with the same precautions as others. Plant oils (pennyroyal, eucalyptus, and citronella) and citrus extracts (limonene, linalool) can be toxic to cats.

FOOD BRANDS

The variety of cat foods available is mind-boggling. How can you decide what is best for your cat? Should you get gourmet canned food, pet-store premium cat food, or a grocery-store brand? What's the difference between inexpensive generic cat food and those deluxe brands?

It is impossible to list every cat food that is acceptable for your cat. Even if we did so, another new food would be produced next week. You and your veterinarian should discuss your cat's diet and decide what food is best.

Ask your veterinarian about his or her experience with various brands of food. Many vets will push a particular brand that they sell. These are usually "premium" foods that are good for your cat but not always essential for his health. If you can't afford a premium food, ask your vet for another recommendation. Other foods may be just fine for your cat.

Of course, you should follow your vet's instructions if a therapeutic diet is prescribed for your cat's health. Also, take heed of veterinarians' warnings about problems they have seen with any specific brand of food.

You don't have to pay the extra cost of premium foods as long as your cat is healthy and has no special dietary requirements. Don't go to the opposite extreme, though, and buy the cheapest food. Stick with major name brands and avoid generic foods.

Generic, inexpensive foods contain lower-quality ingredients. Sometimes the food has never been tested by feeding trials (feeding it to real cats); instead, the company just has to show that the food contains minimum amounts of certain ingredients. That's not a good way to tell if the food is adequate for a real cat. For instance, a high protein level is useless if the amino acid balance is incorrect. The total amount of protein listed may not be digested or absorbed. To be sure your cat's diet has been proven with feeding studies, check the label, ask your veterinarian, or write to the company.

Comparing the costs of various foods by weight can be misleading. That's because each food contains a different density of nutrients. Your cat will eat enough to maintain his weight, or if the food tastes good, he might eat too much and gain weight. To find out the real cost of the food you feed, note the date and price of the food on the bag when it is opened. When the bag is finished, divide the number of days into the cost to get the price per day. Compute canned food costs similarly.

Should you change foods occasionally? It is fine to feed one diet if it's well balanced and nutritious. Some veterinarians recommend changing food brands or flavors as a way of insuring the cat gets a varied, balanced diet. Other proponents of the change-food-often theory want to avoid a finicky cat. Yet many cats never become finicky and will eat a new food even if they've had the same diet for some time. (See "Feeding Finicky Cats.")

Some cats must eat low-calorie ("diet") foods or foods made

to prevent urinary disorders. In that case, it is not a good idea to change foods. If your cat is fed a therapeutic diet, feed only the food your vet recommends for your cat's health.

FOOD LABELS

Smart consumers like you will read the label on their cat's food. Before you begin to consider the ingredients, take a general look at the food. What can the label tell you? First, be sure the food is appropriate for your cat's age and weight.

Kittens up to six to twelve months need to eat kitten food, not cat food. Look for a label that says "kitten," "growth," or "for all life stages." You can begin to offer food to kittens when they are four weeks old. Moisten a small amount and place it in a shallow pan for the kittens. Pregnant and nursing mother cats also should be fed kitten food.

Adult cats need either diet or regular ("maintenance") cat food. The label should state "complete and balanced." Although these foods are tested as adequate for adult cats, some experts feel that present testing methods are inadequate. These nutritionists recommend feeding foods labeled "complete and balanced *for all life stages*" to adult cats as well as to kittens, since the testing requirements for growth are more stringent.

Foods labeled "dinner" or "platter" are not necessarily balanced—be sure their labels include the words "complete and balanced." "Gourmet" foods are *not* meant for daily feeding and may not meet a cat's nutrient requirements.

Now look at the guaranteed analysis and list of ingredients. Unfortunately, the guaranteed analysis on a cat food label shows only the minimum or maximum amounts of certain ingredients. That information is practically useless in telling you whether the food is acceptable for your cat.

Two cat foods with identical guaranteed analysis labels can be drastically different. That's because the analysis doesn't show the *quality* of the nutrients in the food. For instance, protein itself won't do any good unless the amino acid balance is correct for your cat. So comparing the guaranteed analysis among different foods isn't a useful way to determine which one is best.

Besides the guaranteed analysis, your cat's food also has a list of ingredients. You can compare foods within a class (canned vs. canned) but not between classes (dry vs. canned) based on the ingredient label. That's because canned foods have higher water content, which alters the way ingredients are listed.

As a general rule, there should be at least one animal-based protein source within the first two ingredients on canned food and within the first three ingredients on dry food. But cereal ingredients aren't bad in themselves. In fact, it is important that the food contains more than just meat. A strictly meat-based diet lacks nutrients essential for your cat's health.

Don't choose the food whose label has the most ingredients or the highest level of certain nutrients. Although you may think your cat is getting better nutrition, it's important to realize that optimal health depends on both minimum *and maximum* levels of each nutrient. An excess of some nutrients can interfere with absorption of others.

What about "ash content"? Urinary problems are not related to the ash content of food. Cats with urinary disorders need a food that is specifically low in magnesium and that promotes an acid urine. The ash level includes all minerals, and low ash doesn't always mean low magnesium.

Finally, look for a statement telling how the food was tested. You want a food that has been tested by feeding it to real cats, not by laboratory analysis alone. Search for the words "substantiated by feeding studies" or "tested with feeding trials" on the label.

You may be interested in feeding your cat a "natural" or

"organic" cat food. Beware of these words on cat food labels. Many companies take advantage of your good intentions by labeling foods "natural," but there is no legal definition of that word. What is "natural" to a cat food company may be entirely different from what you think of as natural.

The phrase "no added preservatives" also can be deceiving. This claim can be made if no preservatives are added to the ingredients when the cat food is formulated. But there can be preservatives *already in* some of the ingredients. This commonly occurs when fat already containing BHA/BHT is used in "natural foods." When you feed preservative-free foods, be sure the food is dated and that you use it before its expiration.

If you want to feed a natural or organic food, write to the company and ask specifically why its food is labeled that way. Then you can be sure you are getting what you had in mind.

It is important that you read your cat food label, but you can see that you can't rely on only that information to decide what food is best for your cat. To be safe, use major name-brand foods from companies that test their foods with feeding trials. Then listen to your veterinarian's recommendations. Your cat should fare well.

FOOD TYPES

Which is better, canned or dry food? What about the semimoist varieties? Sometimes what your cat likes best isn't what is best for him.

In the past, consumers were scared away from dry food when it was thought to be the cause of urinary disorders in cats. We now know that urinary disorders are caused by a combination of other factors. Whether a cat's food is wet or dry has little effect on the problem.

Dry foods are cost-effective, nutritious, and flavorful. They are the best choice for most situations. Chewing dry food *might* help keep tartar off your cat's teeth (don't depend on it, though). You can leave dry food out all day without fuss. Cats are natural nibblers, eating twelve to twenty meals each day. Dry food allows cats to enjoy this normal eating behavior. However, some cats take this to an extreme and nibble to obesity. There is nothing wrong with measuring out your cat's daily portion of dry food rather than just keeping the bowl full.

Many cats prefer canned food. But cats shouldn't eat all the canned food they want. Measure your cat's meals to keep him trim. Canned food costs more than dry, and since it will spoil, it cannot be left in the cat's bowl for more than a few hours.

Canned food is a good choice if your cat has a poor appetite, is too thin, or is nursing kittens. The good taste will encourage your cat to eat well and take in that extra needed nutrition. You also may choose to keep a few cans of cat food around for special treats. But cats do not have a nutritional requirement for canned food.

Semimoist food is appealing because it doesn't have to be refrigerated yet is soft like canned food. It has disadvantages, though: It's often expensive, bad for the teeth, and fattening. In addition, semimoist foods are loaded with preservatives. One of those is propylene glycol, which may be harmful to the cat's red blood cells. Manufacturers are now changing their recipes to omit this additive.

When you compare various food labels, it may appear that canned foods contain more meat than dry foods. That's not always the case. If ingredients are listed on an "as-is" basis in canned food, the meat will come first because it contains more water than cereal—even when the food contains more cereal than meat. For a real comparison, you must compare ingredients of all foods on a dry-matter basis.

What about a home-made diet for your cat? Many people

prefer to know exactly what their cats are eating. Yet cats have specific and unusual dietary requirements, and it is easy to feed them an improper diet. Cats need high levels of fat and protein. Don't guess at your cat's dietary needs. If you choose this method, be sure you get a recipe for a balanced cat diet from your veterinarian.

Some cats are given a prescription for a special diet. Therapeutic diets can ease the signs of heart disease, kidney failure, or diabetes. Others are made for cats with allergies, urinary tract disease, or intestinal disorders. Several companies now make these diets, and even more companies make diet or "light" cat foods.

Each diet is formulated specifically for certain conditions, with adjustments made in the minerals, protein type and amount, and other ingredients. Your veterinarian must perform diagnostic tests to determine which diet, if any, is best for your cat. Once a special diet is prescribed, then your cat should eat *only* that food. Home-made recipes that mimic the commercial diet are available too.

Do not add any other dry or canned commercial cat food or give treats to a cat on a prescription diet. Just one piece of a commercially available cat treat may have too much salt or protein for your cat's condition. If you want to give your cat a treat, ask your vet what type is acceptable.

Therapeutic diets work best when they are given at the earliest stages of disease. You won't usually notice illness at this early stage, so it's important that your cat is examined regularly by a veterinarian. Yearly checkups allow your vet to spot potential problems. Older cats require blood tests to discover disease before it becomes severe.

What about hypoallergenic diets? Cats can be allergic to certain ingredients in their food. But cats don't show signs the same way you might expect. Most cats with food allergy have itchy skin. Other cats are simply intolerant to certain foods, developing diarrhea or vomiting when they eat that food. That's technically not an allergy, but the solution is the same—change foods.

Changing foods is not as simple as changing flavors or brands. Your cat could be allergic to any ingredient, but the most common ones are dairy products, fish, and beef. Additives also can cause allergic reactions.

Lamb-and-rice diets, which have been used in cases of food allergy (see "Itching"), are becoming fashionable. Many cat food companies responded to this demand by making foods labeled "lamb and rice" or "hypoallergenic," but a close inspection of the label often reveals a variety of potentially allergenic ingredients.

There's nothing wrong with selecting a lamb-based diet for your cat, but consider it in the same light as choosing liver or beef flavor. If your cat has a health problem or allergy, your vet will prescribe the correct diet and give you specific instructions about feeding her.

GARBAGE CAN RAIDING

Does your cat have the bad habit of raiding the garbage can while you are away? Because your cat could be injured or become ill if she tries to eat certain items in your trash, this problem doesn't allow for much training time.

Purchase a covered garbage bin for your kitchen. The ones with a foot pedal that operates the lid are convenient. They can be purchased at reasonable price at any discount store. Even with the lid, kitty could nudge up the top to grab whatever is lying close at hand. To prevent that, put a rock or other heavy object on the trash can lid when you are not home. When you throw away bones or other trash that could be bad for kitty, wrap them in some paper and push them down into the trash can so they aren't lying loose on top.

Some cats like to get into the bathroom trash and take out your used tissues. They usually just play with the tissues and don't eat them, so the problem is the mess rather than a threat to your cat. You could get lids for all your trash cans, or you could decide to live with the problem, or you could try some training techniques to make kitty stop.

Get a bad-tasting product such as Bitter Apple spray at your pet store or veterinarian's office. Use hot pepper sauce or your own mixture of cayenne and water. Spray that on the tissues in your garbage.

GRASS EATING

Most people think cats eat grass when they are sick or have an upset stomach. Occasionally a cat will eat enough grass that it causes vomiting. That's not usually the case, though. Many healthy cats graze routinely. Eating grass in moderation is not harmful to your cat.

Why do cats eat grass? Maybe they like the taste. Perhaps they're bored. Or maybe they are filling a natural nutrient requirement. To be truthful, no one knows.

If your cat eats grass, be sure that the grass is clean and free of chemicals. Do not allow your cat to graze on a recently fertilized lawn or anywhere that chemicals have been sprayed.

Some people grow grass for their indoor cats to chew on. They use a shallow tray, fill it with an inch or so of clean dirt, and plant grass seed. You also can get a kit with seeds and growing instructions from your pet store. Consider growing cat-nip for your cat to eat too.

GROOMING BASICS

"Mrreeow!" Remus protested as I tugged on a snarl. Yet he stayed still as I brushed through his thick white coat. Remus comes running at the sight of his brush because he loves being groomed. He rubs his head against the brush, helping himself to a head scratch. Then he bats at the brush or bites it in frustra-tion when I encounter a mat and pull on his sensitive skin. How about your cat—is it time for brushing?

Cats are low-maintenance pets when it comes to grooming. Yet whether your cat is long-haired or short-haired, a show cat or a couch potato, you need to devote a little time to his groom-ing needs. Frequent brushing reduces shedding. (See "Shedding Excessively: Hairballs" for more tips on that problem.) Groom-ing also allows you to examine your cat for any problems before they become severe. Most cats love being groomed, but yours may need a little training before you can get the job done.

Unfortunately, some cats are so resistant to being groomed that you can't do the job yourself. Others need more frequent grooming than you are able to give. That's why groomers exist. Use your groomer regularly rather than waiting for kitty's coat to become a matted mess.

Do-it-yourselfers need these basic grooming tools: brush, comb, and nail trimmers. Optional accessories include electric clippers to remove mats, a flea comb to remove fleas, and kitty shampoo for bathing your cat.

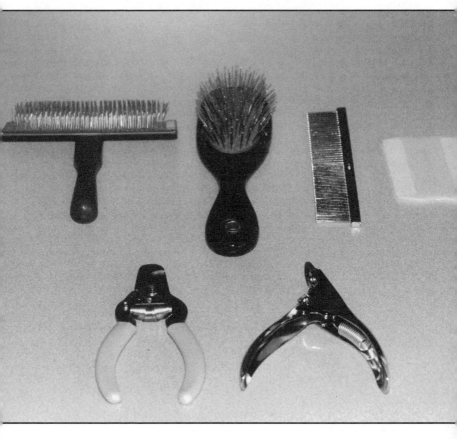

Basic grooming tools

Short-haired cats only need the dirt brushed out of their coats now and then. A longer coat must be brushed or combed regularly to prevent mats. Set aside a few minutes once a week to groom your cat. Brush daily in shedding season.

Start slowly if your cat resists being groomed. Use a small brush that you can hold in the palm of your hand, and just pet your cat with the brush. Stay away from sensitive areas for the first few sessions. You want kitty to think of grooming as a pleasant experience.

Eventually your cat will come running at the sight of the brush. Now you can slowly move onto sensitive areas, such as the belly and under the tail. Brush the chin or another area that kitty really likes, then take a short soft stroke on his belly, then go back to the chin. Gradually kitty will realize that brushing his belly doesn't hurt and that he will be brushed in other wonderful places in between those more sensitive areas.

You may need someone to hold your cat while you brush his rear end. Have your handler restrain your cat by grasping him at the scruff of the neck, without lifting the cat. Most cats will lie quietly on their sides while being restrained by a scruff hold. The scruff hold is simply to keep kitty in one place while you gently brush under his tail.

Clip the rear end of long-haired cats to prevent feces from sticking. Use blunt-tipped scissors to trim the hair around the anus and the underside of the tail to about a half-inch long.

Long-haired cats may be more comfortable in the hot summer months if they are given a haircut. One popular cut is the "lion's cut," which leaves hair around the face and a tuft of hair at the tip of the tail. The body hair is clipped to a length of about one inch. This cut should be done in the beginning of summer to allow plenty of time for kitty to grow back a full coat for winter. Don't laugh at your cat and he won't feel embarrassed.

Long-haired breeds are prone to developing hair mats under the elbows and around the rear end. Even though the cat grooms himself religiously, mats still develop. The best way to prevent mats is to brush your cat at least once a week, if not daily. Some people use a little cornstarch on their brush to reduce matting.

Dry, flyaway hair tends to mat more. Run a humidifier in your home to see if that helps. Also, mats occur more during shedding season, so brush kitty more often then.

In spite of all your efforts, an occasional mat will develop. Use a comb to untangle small mats. You will need clippers or scissors to remove larger ones. Clippers allow removal of hair close to the skin. If you don't have clippers, carefully use blunt-tipped scissors to clip out the mat. Be sure you can see the skin so you won't accidentally cut the cat.

While you're grooming kitty, check for scabs, sores, or hair loss. Cats are very susceptible to abscesses, a type of infection that follows small bites or scratches. You can avoid this problem if you find minor injuries early and keep them clean. Also look for flea dirt or fleas.

Some cats have excess tears that continually drip down the face. Normal tears should exit from the eye through the tear duct, which empties into the nose. Short-nosed cats, such as the Persian, have smaller tear ducts than normal. They also have less area in the eyelid for tears to accumulate. The result is that tears spill over onto the face.

Keep the area around the eyes clean by wiping it with a soft, damp cloth. See your veterinarian if the discharge is coming from only one eye, the eyes are red, the cat squints, or the discharge becomes thick.

Don't forget to look in your cat's ears. The inside of the ear should be whitish-pink and clean. There may be a small amount of wax, but it shouldn't obscure your view. If the ear is red, itchy, smelly, or contains brownish material, then your cat should be examined by a veterinarian. Don't use a pet-store remedy, since treatments vary and will depend on the cause of the problem. For instance, a bacterial infection won't get better with ear mite medicine.

What if you want to clean the ear? Mild ear cleansers for cats are available from veterinarians and pet stores. Squirt the cleanser into the ear, massage the base of the ear, then wipe out the ear canal with a tissue. Don't insert cotton swabs into the ear, since you could just push debris farther in or injure the eardrum.

Cats rarely have a continual problem with oily or dirty ears, so you shouldn't have to clean them very often. If you find that you need to clean your cat's ears more than once a month, there is likely to be an infection or ear mites present. (See "Itching.") Take kitty to the vet to find out the cause.

GROOMING PROBLEMS

Cats spend up to one-third of their lives grooming themselves. Cats groom to keep themselves clean, to cool their bodies, and to remove loose hair. Cats sweat only through their paws, but they create a cooling effect by wetting their hair. Cats also groom as a friendly social behavior. Some cats groom themselves when they are frightened, puzzled, or embarrassed.

Since cats do so well at self-bathing, it is unusual for them to develop scruffy or dirty coats. When a cat doesn't groom herself normally, something is wrong.

How can you keep your cat's coat sleek, full, and shiny? A healthy coat must grow from the inside. Be sure you are feeding your cat a good-quality food with a minimum of table scraps or treats. Cats that eat too much dog food or that are fed a cheap, poor-quality food will have a poor hair coat.

If your cat's coat doesn't look good, then she could be sick. Once you have checked the food quality the next step is a veter-

Cats spend up to one-third of their lives grooming.

inary checkup. Do this first, not last—your cat's condition could worsen while you try countless vitamins or shampoos.

Some cats get dandruff. The most common cause of dandruff is poor-quality food. Dandruff can also be a sign of many illnesses. Another common cause is dry skin. Cats with dry-skin dandruff will look worse in the winter, in houses with forced-air heat or wood stoves. Older cats sometimes get dry, flaky skin too.

Try running a humidifier in the house to see if that helps. Daily brushing will loosen dandruff and stimulate circulation to the skin. There are special shampoos available for cats with dandruff, as well as vitamin supplements that contain ingredients essential for healthy skin. But before you buy a vitamin, be sure you are feeding the correct food. Your veterinarian can help you with these decisions.

All cats love to roll in the dirt. Then they get up, shake off, and unless they are white, they don't look too dirty. You have three choices with this kind of cat: Keep her indoors, let her stay dusty, or bathe and brush her frequently. Chances are that you will come to some sort of compromise among those three alternatives.

"Stud tail" is a condition where the area at the tail head and on the cat's back gets greasy and matted. Male cats get the condition most often because they have more sebaceous skin glands there. Frequent brushing keeps the problem under control. You also can ask your vet for a shampoo that will reduce the oiliness.

HAIR LOSS: BEHAVIORAL CAUSES

There are many causes of hair loss in cats. One of the most frustrating is a psychologic disorder. In these cases, the cat grooms herself excessively out of sheer boredom or as a nervous habit. The result is loss or thinning of hair. The medical term for this syndrome is *psychogenic alopecia.* Your veterinarian will make the diagnosis after examining your cat. (For information about shedding or hairballs, see "Shedding Excessively: Hairballs.")

Psychogenic alopecia may start when a cat licks an area that is painful or irritated. Sometimes, instead, a stressful incident in the cat's life makes her start the excessive grooming. That stress could be the addition of a new person to the household, a change in your job, or moving to a new home. No matter what incident started the behavior, though, it continues as a bad habit.

Any breed of cat can develop psychogenic alopecia, but certain breeds are more commonly affected: Siamese, Himalayan, Abyssinian, and Burmese.

Treatment of a cat with this problem must take two approaches: Resolve the initial cause (the stress), and stop the cycle of excessive grooming. Veterinarians prescribe hormonal or antianxiety drugs to halt the excessive grooming behavior. The vet also will look for any medical cause of the problem. If none is found, then you must make a strong effort to try to find and eliminate the stress in your cat's life.

With psychogenic alopecia, the sooner you begin treatment, the greater your chances of success. You hope to stop the behavior before it becomes an ingrained habit. Medications are given for several months, then tapered off to see if the behavior returns. If the stress has been removed or if your cat has become accustomed to whatever change has occurred, the excessive grooming activity may not resume. Some cats must be on lifelong treatment. Others need to be treated intermittently throughout their lives when a new stressful incident occurs.

Psychogenic alopecia is hard to diagnose, since there is no specific test for the problem. Your cat may groom herself only when you are absent, so don't assume that this isn't a problem just because you haven't noticed the behavior. Other disorders that can look similar include allergy (to food, pollen, or fleas) and *feline endocrine alopecia* (a hormone-responsive disorder).

Cats with allergy will be itchy, but you usually won't see your cat scratch. Itchy cats sometimes just groom themselves excessively. All you may notice is hair loss—the same thing you would see with many other disorders. (See "Itching.")

Endocrine alopecia is thought to be related to sex hormone imbalances. In this disease the hair falls out from the roots. This is different from allergy or psychogenic alopecia, where the cat's excessive grooming causes the hairs to break off. Endocrine alopecia responds to treatment with hormones.

In another form of excessive self-grooming the cat jumps up and seems to attack herself with a sudden burst of biting and licking. (A cat with a flea bite will do so too, but we're talking about a continuous problem.) This syndrome is thought to be a form of epilepsy. It responds well to antiepileptic drugs.

Your vet can examine your cat to determine whether her hair loss is caused by one of these syndromes or something else.

HOLDING A CAT

Everyone knows how to hold a cat. After all, you live with your cat and hold him every day. Only children must be taught how to hold cats, right?

Still, most people have difficulty holding their cat at times. Do you have trouble getting your cat to sit still while you groom him? When you visit the vet, do you have difficulty getting your cat out of his carrier? Does your cat struggle as you lift him onto the table? Part of his discomfort may be in the way you carry him, not a reaction to being at the vet's.

A cat will struggle if his weight is not supported evenly. Cats like to be horizontal when lifted. They will struggle if their back legs dangle. Once a cat has been picked up, all four legs should be supported.

Use both hands to pick up a cat. Put one under the chest just behind the forelegs. Put the other under the belly as far back as you can. Once you have picked up the cat, cradle his hind legs in one arm and let his forelegs rest on the other arm.

Another way to pick up a cat is to reach around behind him and scoop him up. Use this method when the cat is sitting on an elevated surface, such as a table. It also works well with a cat that becomes frightened or aggressive when you approach from above or when you reach toward his face. Use one arm to reach around the cat at the same level as his body. His body should rest on your arm as you scoop him toward you.

You can hold a cat in one arm. The cat's body should rest along your arm with the legs bent in their natural position under the cat. Use your hand to support his front end and front paws, and allow his rear end and rear legs to rest in the crook of your elbow. Check to be sure there aren't any loose legs dangling. Hold the cat against your body so he is supported from the side as well as from below.

Some cats like to be held on your chest facing you, with their paws reaching up to hug you. Use one arm to support the cat's rear end. This hold should be used only with friendly cats.

Lifting by the scruff of the neck should be reserved for small kittens. Although you should not lift an adult cat by the scruff of his neck (that's too much weight to suspend from the skin!), you can use the "scruff hold" to help restrain the cat when necessary. Use your fist to grasp a large fold of skin directly behind the cat's ears. Do not lift the cat or he will struggle.

The scruff hold is ideal for extracting cats out of small spaces when you can't reach the whole cat. Reach over the cat, grasp the scruff of his neck, and slide him out. Also use the scruff hold to restrain your cat gently while you groom him.

Towel holds are great for medicating cats. You can wrap your cat in a towel to keep his claws away. Another special hold is the between-the-legs technique. Kneel in a corner facing outward, with your cat between your knees and facing away from you. The cat can't go backward or sideways, so you only have to keep him from going forward.

Small children should always sit down before they hold a cat. They can get scratched if they try to pick up the cat. Even if the cat is too polite to scratch, and he endures being dangled or squeezed, it isn't very nice for him. Until children are able to pick up and hold the cat horizontally in their arms, they should sit down first.

HOT WEATHER AND OVERHEATING

While cats are more resistant to heat problems than are dogs, they certainly aren't immune. And the problem is not limited to the southern states. Could your cat ever suffer from heat exhaustion or heatstroke?

While you are able to get relief from the sun, your cat is forced to deal with the environment that you create. Problems with heat aren't limited to extremely hot days. Heatstroke could occur if your cat doesn't drink enough water and can't get out of the sun. High humidity will increase the chances of heat exhaustion. Trouble also occurs when a cat is confined in a small area with poor ventilation, such as a car.

Cats left in a car could suffer from heatstroke. On a summer day with an outside temperature of 85 degrees, the temperature in your car can reach 102 degrees in ten minutes, 120 degrees in thirty minutes—even with the windows cracked open.

Cats release body heat by sweating and panting. Unlike people, cats do not sweat through their skin. The foot pads are one area that have sweat glands. Some cooling occurs when cool air flows over the body. Cats that get too hot release heat by panting. Panting by itself is not a serious sign, but it should signal you that the cat needs to move to a cooler area.

Signs of heat exhaustion or stroke include panting, weakness, vomiting, and diarrhea. The cat may go into convulsions or fall into a coma. The brain, heart, and kidneys may receive permanent damage.

Breeds with short noses such as the Persian have more difficulty breathing than most and may be more susceptible to heatstroke. Elderly cats also may be at higher risk. They are less mobile, less fit, and less able to regulate their body heat. The older cat's kidneys are prone to damage from dehydration.

Overweight cats have a higher risk of heatstroke. Also, any cat that is taking medication could be prone to trouble. For instance, some tranquilizers can disrupt the cat's natural heat regulation.

How can you determine whether your cat is having trouble tolerating the heat? First, lift your cat's lip to look at the color of the gums. Normal mucous membranes are light pink. Press your finger into the gum and note the white spot that refills with pink color within a second or two. With heatstroke, the gums become dark red and the refill time is prolonged.

A rectal thermometer is an essential item in your "cat cupboard." Your cat's body temperature, normally 101 to 102 degrees Fahrenheit, can rise to over 106 degrees with heatstroke. The cat with heatstroke must be cooled immediately with water and taken to a veterinarian. (Use water from your hose or cold water faucet, not ice water.)

You can prevent problems with the heat. While you are driving with your cat, leave the air conditioner on or the window open slightly to allow a breeze. Stop frequently during long drives to allow your cat to drink. Leash-train your cat so you can let her out for fresh air during long trips. Consider driving at night and sleeping during the daytime if you plan a long trip during hot weather.

If you must drive during hot weather and your auto is not air-conditioned, wrap an ice pack in a towel and place that in the cat's carrier. If it is extremely hot, wet down the cat occasionally. Consider a body clip for long-haired cats in the summer.

HUNTING

Some people want their cats to catch mice. Others would rather their cats didn't kill mice or birds. Both will be discussed here.

Cats learn to catch mice from their mother. If left to her own instincts, a mother cat will catch small prey and bring it to the kittens. She may leave the prey alive and allow the kittens to play with it, as a sort of hunting practice. As the kittens grow older, they watch their mother hunt and mimic her actions. Kittens usually will hunt for the same type of prey that they saw their mother bring to them.

Even without this training, some cats will learn to catch mice on their own. You have about a 50 percent chance that any cat will become a good hunter. But if you want a for-sure mouser, you should get a kitten whose mother is a mouser too. Remember, though, that a barn kitten that has not been handled will not become tame easily. If you want a friendly cat that also catches mice, get a kitten that has been handled by people since birth but that has been left with its mouser-mother until it is about twelve weeks old.

It may be a good idea to avoid feeding canned food or any treats in case your cat looks forward to eating those rather than catching mice. But your cat does not have to be starved to encourage her to hunt. Feed dry cat food, and depend on your cat's hunting and play instincts to catch the mice.

Never, never, use mouse or rat poison if you have a cat that catches mice. When a mouse eats the poison and dies, its body can contain enough poison to kill your cat. Hiding the poison doesn't work, since the rodent could crawl out of hiding before it dies. If you want to get rid of more mice than your cat can handle, use mousetraps that are put where the cat can't reach.

Remember that mice can carry tapeworms. A cat that catches mice should be checked regularly for these parasites. (Cats also get tapeworms from fleas.) If your cat gets tapeworms more than once, your vet may recommend treating at regular intervals rather than waiting for signs of the worms to appear.

Other diseases may be picked up from wildlife. For instance, cats in the Southwest may catch rabbits infested with the fleas that carry plague or tularemia, both potentially fatal diseases. Sometimes outdoor cats don't get checked as often as an indoor cat would. If your cat shows any sign of illness, take her to the vet as soon as possible.

What if you *don't* want your cat to catch mice or birds? After all, kitty gets plenty of food. You hate to see those small creatures suffer. Besides, the cat brings body parts into the house and makes a mess.

You can take two approaches to hunting. First, choose a cat that is less likely to hunt. Second, do what you can to prevent or reduce the cat's hunting.

Mother cats teach their kittens not just how to hunt, but what type of prey to catch. For instance, if a kitten was able to watch mice being caught but not birds, it would be less likely to hunt for birds as an adult. To stack the odds in your favor, get a cat whose mother did not catch mice or birds. Then the kitten should not be exposed to birds until it is a year old.

The easiest way to prevent your cat from killing little creatures is not to let her outside. That choice is best for your cat's health anyway.

If your cat must go out, though, you have another alternative. Get a brightly colored, reflective collar with a bell attached. The sight and sound of that collar will warn off most birds. If kitty is so stealthy that she moves without the bell jingling, attach several more bells. If that doesn't work, consider allowing her out only on a leash, under supervision.

Declawing is not a good idea for cats that are allowed out. For one thing, cats without claws may still catch mice and birds. They also are less able to defend themselves against dogs or other predators.

INDOOR CATS

The debate of the outdoor versus indoor cat won't be solved here. Make an educated decision after studying the facts.

Indoor cats are not deprived of any essential "natural" experiences (except injury and illness). Cats fare well in tiny apartments and large homes. Use your common sense and don't overcrowd cats. As a general rule, never keep more cats than there are rooms.

Your cat can enjoy the outdoors without being exposed to danger. Teach kitty to walk on a leash. Provide an outdoor run, screened-in porch, or window seat for your cat to enjoy the outdoors. You also can install a cat door in a window, then construct an enclosed cat run leading from the window out into the backyard.

Still worried that your cat is deprived if not let outdoors? Consider this: It's a fact that outdoor cats don't live as long as indoor cats. In the city, dangers include moving cars and other cats. Outdoor city cats not only endanger themselves, they also annoy neighbors, get into fights, and spread disease. If you live in the city, it is best to never let your cat outdoors.

Country life isn't safe either. Coyotes, roaming dogs, and cars will threaten kitty. No matter how rural your area, there are always stray cats that can spread disease.

The outdoor cat is likely to bring you choice tidbits, such as dead mice and birds. Fleas will be more of a problem, since kitty will be reexposed continually. And you will constantly be pestered to open the door. "Let me in!" and "Let me out!" are perpetual cries. Sometimes it seems as if the cat's entertainment is finding out how many times you will open the door.

Keeping your cat indoors will spare him from danger. Read "Depression, Boredom, and Loneliness," and "Playing and Toys" for tips on keeping the indoor cat entertained. Also see "Outdoor Cats Converted to Indoor Cats."

INTELLIGENCE

Are cats intelligent animals? How smart is your cat? Some people compare the intelligence of cats to dogs, using the example of training to "prove" that dogs are smarter.

The fact that cats can't be trained like dogs only means cats don't think like dogs. For instance, few people train their dogs to use one area as a toilet. Yet we take it for granted that cats

Intelligent cats need stimulating toys.
(Photo courtesy of Gillian's Jungle)

will use a litter box. In fact, some cats are trained to use our toilets! The differences in how cats and dogs can be trained lie in their priorities and motives.

Most "intelligence tests" are designed to see if an animal thinks like a person. They don't necessarily show true intelligence. Since dogs think more like people, they tend to "score" higher than cats.

Your cat can be just as responsive as a dog if you use signals that the cat understands. Your cat can be trained as much as you expect and desire. You don't have to live with bad behavior.

Many of the feline behaviors thought of as "bad" are normal actions for cats. To change the behavior, you must give the cat an alternative rather than using punishment alone. You can train your cat to be good, and you can train him to follow commands. (See "Training Basics" and "Training: Come, Sit, or Fetch.")

Are some breeds smarter than others? There are definite breed personality differences and definite opinions on breed intelligence. Yet few scientific studies have been done to evaluate those differences.

Some people believe that short-haired cats tend to be smarter. Long-haired cats such as the Persian are given less credit for brains and more for a relaxed personality. Siamese are thought to be intelligent as well as demanding. Abyssinians are noted for their intelligence.

Cats have right and left "hands," just as people do. About 40 percent of cats are ambidextrous, another 40 percent are right-pawed, and the rest prefer to use their left paws.

Some science purists attribute all of a cat's actions to instinct. On the other extreme are people who assume human motivations for their cat's actions. The truth is likely to be somewhere in between.

INTRODUCING CATS

Whether you have one cat or several, adding an additional cat to your home can be stressful. What is the best way to introduce the newcomer? How can you reduce conflict?

The first question you may ask about a second cat is whether you should get one. After all, cats are solitary animals. Can cats learn to live together? The answer depends on your specific situation.

It is true that cats are solitary in the wild. But in your home, where food and shelter are plentiful, there is no strong need for a cat to be alone. A second cat can ease your cat's loneliness or provide an outlet for your cat's rambunctious energy.

Cats enjoy having playmates and companions. They often develop close bonds when they live together. Cats sleep together, groom each other, and even greet each other after a prolonged absence.

Getting two kittens at once is easiest. It is easier to introduce a kitten to an adult than to introduce two adults. Adult cats adjust better if they were exposed to a variety of other cats when they were young. (See "Adopting a Cat" for tips on choosing a cat that will get along with others.)

Two adult cats may learn to live together in harmony but may not become as close as those raised together from kittenhood. Whether they can learn to get along depends on their personalities, the size of the house, and the number of other pets. For instance, let's say you already have several cats, including George, a cat with a dominant personality. George might not take kindly to the addition of another dominant cat. On the other hand, two sedate cats that aren't easily ruffled might get along well.

Some cats fight or develop other behavior problems when living with another cat. There is a limit to the number of cats you can have without conflict. One study showed that the

Many older cats will adjust to a new kitten without fuss.

chances of urine spraying (a sign of stress and conflict) steadily increased with the number of cats in a household. With ten cats, spraying was almost certain to occur. Use your common sense and avoid overcrowding your cats.

Neutering (males) and spaying (females) goes a long way toward reducing fights. If your older cat is not yet "fixed," now is the time to do so—before you bring another cat home. If your new kitten is not yet altered, get that done by the time he or she is six months old.

Take your new cat or kitten directly to the vet's office before you ever bring her home. You want to find any contagious disease or parasites right away so you don't infect your other cat. The vet will check for ringworm, ear mites, fleas, leukemia virus, and respiratory virus infections. Once your kitten has a clean bill of health, you can bring her home without worry.

Unless you want to get scratched, don't hold the two cats up nose to nose for an introduction. Instead, put them in separate but adjoining rooms so they can smell each other under the door. Switch their places every day or so, and each will get used to the other's smell.

Let them get together after about a week. Just open the door and ignore them. Let them approach each other at their own speed. If one wants to hide under the couch, let her be. No cat stays under the couch forever. (If you can't bear the wait, close the other cat in a different room and tempt the scaredy-cat out with a treat.)

It's normal to hear some hissing and spitting at first. As long as they do not actually fight, leave the cats to their own devices. You may decide to separate them for part of each day when you are not there to supervise until they've learned to get along.

Don't expect instant friendship. The cats may simply tolerate each other for several months before they will become friends. Be sure to give each cat her own special time for attention and petting. Your relaxed attitude will help them feel secure.

Many times the cats are happiest with a slow introduction. They need time to get used to one another and even more time to become friends. Yet they may be forced together by people who insist they become pals before they are ready. Be patient. You should be able to leave the cats loose in the home together after a few weeks, but it may take months before they become more than tolerant of each other. Don't give up hope that they will become close, because it takes time.

Some people skip the slow introduction and just let the new cat loose in the home. Many cats adjust this way, and many others do not. If your cats are not adjusting well, go back to the technique of rotating them among rooms. Signs that should tell you to ease off on the introductions include not using the litter box, not eating, excessive grooming, hiding constantly, or fighting.

To minimize conflict, each cat should have her own food and water dishes, her own bed, and, in the beginning, her own litter box. (Once they get to be pals, you can go back to one box per two or three cats, assuming you clean it every day.)

After you've had the new kitten or cat for several weeks, and have completed the room-rotation technique, you can try some of the following tips to help the two cats get along. One technique is to get the two cats to smell alike by giving them both a bath with the same shampoo. A variation of this is to get both cats wet and put them in the same room. They will be so busy grooming themselves that they will forget to fight.

Another technique is to keep the cats separated except at mealtime. Feed the cats at opposite ends of the same room. They will be able to see each other but will be occupied with eating. (Cats don't usually fight over food as dogs do.) Eventually they learn to stay in the same room together without conflict.

Playing with both cats at once helps too. Get a long, thick string and attach a soft toy to either end. Rub catnip on the toys. Use the two ends to play with each cat. If one cat decides to pounce on the other, throw the toy at her to deflect the attack.

Does getting a second cat sound like too much work? Most of

the time you won't have to use all of the techniques mentioned here. They are all included because certain methods work with certain cats. You will learn through trial and error which method works best for you. Many, many people have several cats that all get along. After their introductory hisses, most cats become playmates and friends.

If you aren't sure whether your cat would tolerate sharing her home, discuss your cat's personality with your vet. Find out whether another cat would fit in and what personality to look for. (See "Adopting Your Special Cat" and "Fighting Cats" for more tips.)

INTRODUCING CATS TO DOGS

Cats and dogs can be friends. This is proven by thousands of households where they live in harmony. Yet that doesn't mean you can just throw them together without introduction. A little preparation goes a long way toward insuring peace.

Do you already have a dog, and you are going to adopt a cat? A kitten will adjust to your dog more quickly than would a grown cat. If you want to adopt an adult cat, be sure it has been exposed to dogs before.

Confine your dog to the yard or one room of your house on the day you bring your kitten home. Let the cat smell and explore the house without the dog present.

Your dog absolutely must be trained to sit and stay before you bring a cat home. The first several times you put the two in a room together, ask your dog to stay and then let the cat into the room. Allow the cat to approach or not approach the dog as she becomes comfortable doing so.

Cats and dogs can be playmates and friends.

If your dog won't stay in one place, consider using a child's gate in a doorway between rooms to keep the dog from approaching the cat, or close the dog in another room. Put your dog on a leash during those times the two are in the same room together.

Don't leave a small kitten with a dog unattended, no matter how certain you are that the dog won't cause harm. Accidents do happen, even though the dog is just playing.

Sometimes the cat is the bully and the dog ends up getting scratched. Clip your cat's nails and keep the two separate unless you are there to supervise. Is the dog inciting the cat to anger, or is the cat attacking the dog? If the dog is bothering the cat, then you have some dog training to do. (Go back to the sit and stay commands, allowing the two in the same room only when the dog is under control.) If the cat is attacking the dog, then get your water bottle and noisemaker. (See "Discipline and Disobedience.") Squirt the cat if she gets too rough with your dog.

Perhaps you already have a cat, and you are considering whether to get a dog. You wonder whether your cat will be upset forever. Never fear: The two can learn to get along. It will take a bit longer if your adult cat has never been around dogs before.

It's best to get a puppy rather than an adult dog for the easiest transition for your cat. The cat won't be as threatened by the dog's small size, and puppies haven't learned bad habits, such as chasing cats.

Confine the cat in one room while you let the puppy explore your house. Then confine the puppy and let the cat out to smell the new pet. Crate training your pup allows the cat to roam the house as usual while the pup is safely out of the way. (With crate training, the pup is kept in a crate while you sleep or are away, thus discouraging house soiling and mischief making; ask your vet for details.)

After a few days of keeping them separate, allow the puppy and the cat into the same room together. Chances are that the cat will hide under the couch or jump up on a table, hissing and spitting. Just ignore the two and allow them to approach each other as they become ready. If the pup is too rambunctious or chases the cat mercilessly, the pup should be kept on a leash.

Be sure to take your puppy to obedience training as soon as it is old enough. Teach the puppy to sit and stay, and your cat will learn that she is safe when you give the dog the stay command. Then she can come out and get as close to the puppy as she desires. Obedience training also will help your puppy learn that it is not acceptable to chase cats.

The "get-acquainted" time for your pets is just as hard on you as it is on them. Try not to interfere too much, and allow them to get to know each other at their own pace. Each pet needs a place it can feel safe without having you insist that it come out and join the group. (They all will, eventually.)

No matter which pet is the new addition, be sure the cat has somewhere she can escape from the dog. Provide a cat tree or other easily accessible high place in every room that both the cat and the dog may enter. If kitty is allowed in a room where the dog is not, install a cat door that is either too small or too high up for the dog to access. Also set aside a special "cat time" where the dog is confined and the cat has the run of the house.

Keep each pet's food separate where the other can't get at it. Stealing food may lead to fighting. Dogs and cats also have very different nutritional requirements, so eating the other's food isn't good for them. Don't expect any dog, no matter how well trained, to learn to ignore a bowl of cat food that is within easy reach. Put the cat food bowls up high or in a room closed off to the dog.

INTRODUCING CATS TO NEW PEOPLE

Whether it's your fiancé or a new roommate, a new person in the household can disrupt your cat's peace of mind. For the person joining a household with a cat, the transition may be as difficult as taking on a stepchild. Yet most people don't anticipate any problem and are taken aback when conflict occurs. Introducing a cat to a new baby is discussed under "Children and Cats," while adult introductions are discussed here.

Whether your cat dislikes your roommate or vice versa, the first thing to do is give it some time. Don't try to force a close relationship, but let them come together on their own terms. Be patient with your roommate, who perhaps feels "ganged up on" by you and the cat.

A new person in the house often asks that the "cat rules" be changed. Perhaps your cat has always slept with you, but your fiancé wants her out of the bedroom. Or you've always let the cat on the dining table, but your roommate won't allow that.

Try to compromise in the interest of keeping the peace. The transition period may be difficult, but once the changes are enforced consistently, your cat will adjust without hardship. Your roommate needs to feel as if he has a little control over the situation and isn't having his life ruled by the cat.

Sit down with your roommate and make a list of "household rules" for your cat. Is the cat allowed on the table and counter-tops, or in the bedroom? Will the cat sleep with you? It doesn't matter what you decide, but that you make decisions and stick with them.

Perhaps you will agree to keep the cat off the kitchen counter if your roommate doesn't mind the cat on the table. You promise to clean the litter box every day if your fiancé allows the box to stay in the bathroom. Decide how you will enforce the new rules and what kind of discipline is acceptable.

Then stick to the rules and be ready for an adjustment period. If your cat was formerly allowed in the bedroom, she will raise a fuss at bedtime when she's shut out. Make a special kitty bed in another place so your cat has somewhere cozy to sleep. (See "Sleeping" for tips.) You may lose some sleep for a few weeks while kitty meows outside the bedroom, but peace will eventually prevail.

If your cat is no longer allowed on the dining table, use a water bottle to squirt her when she jumps up. Don't feel sorry for kitty and let her up when your roommate isn't home. That will just confuse the cat and prolong the training period.

Sometimes a cat will begin to misbehave when a new person joins the household. Your cries of "She never did that before!" aren't always believed. Explain that the cat is having trouble adjusting and that this bad behavior is not a permanent problem. Having your roommate feed the cat may help.

A shy or timid cat may have difficulty adjusting to a new person in the house. The cat may hide all the time or may hiss and spit when the person approaches. To ease this problem, the new person should be the only one to feed the cat. Have the person sit in the room while the cat eats. He may need to sit far away before the cat will relax enough to eat, and he should not approach the cat. (See "Shy, Timid, or Fearful Cats" for more tips.)

Your cat might have a little trouble adjusting to the new situation, but if you are consistent and persistent then things will soon settle down. Give kitty lots of attention to show that you still love her. Set aside time every day for loving and playing. At the same time, let your roommate and your cat approach each other on their own terms. Give it several months. The two soon will become friends.

ITCHING

A constantly scratching cat is not only miserable, but her scratching behavior becomes annoying to you. Itchy cats might scratch themselves, groom excessively, or both. Itching is most often due to ear mites, fleas, and/or allergy.

Your first step, then, is to take kitty to the vet to find out why she is scratching. All of these problems are treatable, but none is easy to treat.

You usually can tell if your cat is scratching her ears. Sometimes, though, the cat will scratch her neck just as much as her ears. That leaves you with the mistaken impression that she has a skin problem and not an itchy ear.

Ear mites can be difficult to treat. That's partly because dogs and cats pass the mites among themselves. Also, most people don't treat their cat long enough, so the mites return.

You may need to treat your cat for up to six weeks before the problem is truly gone. Ear mites can live outside of the cat's ears too. When the cat curls up to sleep, the mites may crawl out onto her back or tail. Use a flea powder or spray to kill the mites on the cat's body at the same time you use the ear medication given to you by the vet. All your pets must be treated even if they show no signs.

Fleas are easy to see, and you may think they are easy to treat —at first. The main reason people think that flea products don't work is they don't treat the cat, the house, and the yard all at the same time, and repeatedly. Those adult fleas on your cat are just a small fraction of the total number of fleas in your home. Without killing the immature fleas, you will never catch up. Ask your vet for a complete flea control program and then stick with it. (See "Fleas.")

Allergies are another cause of an itchy cat. Cats can be allergic to food, fleas, pollen, dust mites, or other substances. Although most people associate inhalant allergies with respiratory signs, cats can develop itchy skin from this problem. Likewise, cats with food allergies will not necessarily show signs of intestinal upset, but may develop itchy skin.

When an allergy occurs year-round with the same severity, it is most likely due to food or house dust. Cats with allergies to pollen or fleas are worse during certain seasons of the year.

The best way to treat an allergy is to find and remove the cause. A cat with a flea allergy should be kept indoors where the fleas are more easily controlled. Food allergy is treated by feeding a hypoallergenic diet. (Use something recommended by your vet, since commercial "hypoallergenic" diets aren't always hypoallergenic.)

Steroids will make the cat stop scratching, but should be used only to help ease severe signs or when the cause can't be eliminated. Fortunately, cats don't suffer from as many side effects from steroids as do other animals.

In other cases a cat may seem to have a sudden itchy or painful spot. The cat will jump up and lick or bite one area on her body. If this occurs frequently and fleas are not the cause, the problem may not be on the skin at all. Some of these cats have a mental disorder or a mild form of epilepsy. Medication will ease the signs.

Anal rubbing is a sign of an itchy or irritated anus and is not always a sign of worms. One frequent cause is inflamed anal sacs (the glands just inside the anus). Take your cat plus a fresh stool sample to your veterinarian to find the cause of anal rubbing.

KITTEN HYPERACTIVITY

You are sitting on the couch minding your own business when your kitten comes flying through the air at breakneck speed. She leaps onto the couch, attacks your shoelace, catapults from there to the recliner, looks around as if she's seen a ghost, then disappears in a flash around the corner.

Is your cat normal, or is this hyperactivity something to be concerned about? How can you get your kitten to behave more sedately?

Normal kitten behavior often gives people a fright. You might be sitting calmly one minute and have a kitten on your head the next.

You can't stop your cat's playful behavior. Using punishment alone will backfire. Yet you can prevent your cat from damaging household objects or hurting people. (See "Attacking People" and "Biting, Scratching, and Clawing People" for methods to deal with a cat that bites, scratches, or pounces on you in "play.")

The best you can hope for is to channel that energy elsewhere. Two choices are to get another kitten, to give your kitten toys, or both. Movable toys are best. Try a ball or a stuffed mouse suspended on an elastic cord. Play with your cat several times a day. Initiate play with a toy at those times you can predict your cat is about to "cut loose."

To stop your kitten from keeping you awake all night, schedule a rigorous playtime just before bed. Then hope that the kitten will be too tired to pounce on you in your sleep. Consider closing the kitten out of your bedroom at night. Then just be glad your kitten is normal and healthy.

KNEADING AND RUBBING ON PEOPLE

Most cats like to touch people. Chances are you have seen your cat twining herself around someone's legs, rubbing her face against your hand, or sitting on your lap kneading contentedly. Most cat owners interpret these behaviors as different forms of affection. Yet that behavior is more complex than just a friendly interaction.

Cats use scent as one method of communication. The cheeks, chin, and base of the tail have more sebaceous glands than the rest of the cat's body. Sebaceous glands secrete body oils with the cat's odor. Those areas are the ones that cats most like to be scratched or rubbed. When a cat rubs her cheek on a chair or your legs, she leaves a bit of her scent there.

No matter what "instinctive" reason scientists give for the behavior, it is clear that cats love to be petted and scratched. Your cat's rubbing on you is likely her way of telling you where she'd like to be petted.

Sometimes a particularly outgoing cat will seem to rub the most on a person who doesn't like cats. It is possible that the cat senses the person's feelings and "retaliates" by leaving her scent all over that person. The cat may go farther and also urinate on the person's clothing.

A female cat in heat will rub and roll on you or whatever else is in sight. If your six-month-old kitten has suddenly gotten "extra friendly," take her to the vet to be spayed before she gets pregnant.

Kneading behavior has different roots. Kittens knead their mother's belly to stimulate milk letdown into the teats. It is likely that adult cats knead when they are as contented as they had been as kittens. Perhaps the surface they knead upon reminds them of their mother's belly.

Kittens that are weaned too early may knead and suck on fabric. This behavior usually goes away as the kitten grows. You can discourage it the same way a mother cat weans her kittens. Lift the kitten by the scruff of the neck, say "No," and put him down away from the object on which he was sucking or chewing. (See "Chewing and Sucking.")

LEASH TRAINING

Leash training can be invaluable for your cat. Even if you never take your cat outdoors, it is helpful to have him on a leash at other times—for instance, while you are training him to sit or while you are giving him a bath.

Walking your cat on a leash is not the first step, though. First you must get him accustomed to a collar. You may choose between a neck collar and a harness-type collar. Harness collars won't slip off and are best for walking your cat. An H-shaped harness is more comfortable than a figure-8 harness.

A neck collar should be left on your cat at all other times, simply because kitty needs his ID tag in case he ever becomes lost. For an everyday collar, some people prefer a quick-release or safety collar. These are made with elastic or with a Velcro fastener to prevent the cat from becoming entrapped or choking should the collar become caught in something. You should not use quick-release collars for walking on a leash since that might allow kitty to escape in the midst of a walk.

Leaving a collar too loose is not being kind. A loose collar may become caught on something or will fall off. The collar or harness should be snug. You should just be able to fit two fingers under it. A neck collar should not be able to slide over your cat's ears.

Put the harness on kitty and leave it there for a week before you attach the leash. If your cat normally wears a neck collar and you will use the harness only for walking, place the harness on for several hours each day. Give your cat lots of petting and praise while he wears the harness. If it seems to bother him a lot, then feed him a special treat to distract his attention from the harness.

Once kitty is accustomed to the harness, clip on a light leash and let it dangle. Keep kitty in one room under supervision so he doesn't get tangled up in anything.

Practice putting the leash on and letting kitty do what he wants for a week or so. Then pick up the end of the leash. Don't pull on it, just follow your cat wherever he walks. Do this for a few more sessions until he gets used to that too.

Now you reach your biggest challenge. Can you get kitty to follow you? Start in the house, not outside. Get a handful of treats, attach the leash, and take a step away. Call kitty in your most happy voice, give a *tiny* tug on the leash, release the tug, and hold out the treat. As soon as kitty comes toward you, give him the treat.

Never pull on the leash or drag your cat. It won't work. Only positive reinforcement, lots of praise, petting, and an occasional treat will work. It is easy to forget to ease up on the leash, so make a conscious effort at looking for slack in the leash.

Once you have kitty following you around the house, you are ready for the outdoors. When you make the transition from indoors to outdoors, you may have to take a step backward and once again allow kitty to lead you for a few sessions. Be patient. Start in your yard, with the goal of having kitty follow you to all four corners. Keep your sessions short, and stop if you or kitty seems to be getting frustrated. Get a fresh start the next day.

LITTER BOX AIM IS OFF

The poor-aim problem comes in several different varieties. Some cats go into the box and then hang their rear ends out the side. Other cats are too big for the box. Sometimes a cat doesn't like the litter but has good intentions, so he uses the floor near the box. (See "Defecating Out of the Litter Box" or "Urinating Outside the Box" for tips on litter aversion.)

Take a look at your litter box. Watch kitty while he uses the box. Is he too big? Would it help to get a larger box or one with higher sides?

Get a covered box for cats that tend to hang out over the side. Sometimes the cat will still hang out of the single opening, but at least that concentrates the problem in one area.

You may have to retrain your cat to use a new litter box. The cat may feel uncomfortable with a covered box. If he goes to the box and meows, take the lid off to let him use it. Then replace the lid so he realizes it is the same box. To be sure he uses the new box when you are not home, leave him closed in the room with the new box at first.

Another solution is to put your cat's litter box inside a larger cardboard box. Cut away one side of the cardboard box to allow entry. Place newspapers on the floor of the cardboard box. Then replace the newspaper as it becomes soiled.

LITTER BOX AVOIDANCE

Litter box problems rate as the number-one behavior problem in cats. If your cat doesn't have good toilet manners, you are not alone. Your approach to your cat's house soiling should consider two aspects of the problem. First, what type of problem is occurring? Is your cat urinating, spraying, or defecating? (See "Urine Spraying" for ways to tell the difference.)

Second, what is the cause of the problem? Causes can be psychological or medical. Psychological problems include a break in toilet habits and territorial or sexual marking. Medical causes include diarrhea, bladder irritation or infection (feline urological syndrome, or FUS), and diseases, such as diabetes.

The sooner you tackle a toilet problem, the better are your chances for success. Your cat may have stopped using the box suddenly or may have developed a gradual problem. No matter what the circumstances, it is essential to have your cat examined by your veterinarian immediately. Your vet will help you narrow down the cause and be sure there is no medical problem.

After your cat has been checked by the vet, try some of the suggestions under "Litter Box Training and Type of Litter," "Urinating Outside the Box" and/or "Defecating Out of the Litter Box." *Punishment usually doesn't work to control house soiling.* Instead, you must be a sleuth and unearth the reasons behind your cat's behavior. Once you understand why your cat is soiling the house, then retraining him is much easier. If you aren't successful, consult with your vet again for advice, before your cat's problem becomes a habit.

You may find it difficult to determine which one of your several cats is causing the house-soiling problem. You can't begin to treat or resolve the problem until you know which cat is the culprit. Isolate one cat at a time in one room of the house. Put a litter box and food in there. Endure the plaintive cries to let him out. It's for his own good, and it won't last forever.

Keep your cat's litter box scooped out regularly.

Does the problem stop? Then the isolated kitty is the culprit. If not, let that cat out and put another one in his place. Rotate cats every twenty-four hours until you find the one who has the problem.

LITTER BOX MESS AND SMELL

No one likes walking into a home that has a "cat smell." Owning a cat doesn't have to mean that your house stinks. Start by cleaning feces out of the box daily. Change the litter at least once a week, or more often if you smell an odor.

If you still smell something when the litter box is clean, then it is likely your cat has urinated elsewhere. Get down on your hands and knees and sniff every corner until you find the spot. Then clean it with an odor neutralizer. (See "Odor Control.")

Use deodorized litter if your cat doesn't mind the smell. Some people use alfalfa pellets for litter. You can get alfalfa pellets that are sold as litter, or buy bags that are sold as rabbit or horse feed.

A light dusting of baking soda in the bottom of the litter box, under the litter, may help absorb odors. Use a plastic bag for a litter box liner to reduce the penetration of odors into the box itself. Wash the box with soap and water as necessary to keep it clean and dry.

Covered boxes contain odors nicely. Some of these boxes have a filter in the top that helps to minimize odors. Most cats adapt to using a covered box.

Your cat's food can influence the odor of the feces. If the feces are particularly malodorous, try switching food brands to see if the odor improves. The food also influences the volume of feces. More digestible foods will result in a lower volume of feces.

What about the scattered litter that ends up all over the floor? A covered box will also help minimize this problem, as will a box with high sides. Place a piece of indoor-outdoor carpet, a false-turf mat, or a door mat under the box so that it extends out about a foot on each side. The litter tends to stick to the mat rather than sliding all over the floor. Keep a hand-held, portable vacuum near the litter box so cleanup of scattered litter is easy.

Another solution is to put your cat's litter box inside a larger cardboard box. Cut away one side of the cardboard box to allow entry. Scattered litter will be retained in the cardboard box.

Sometimes a dog causes the litter box mess. Dogs like to eat cat feces. Your dog may leave a trail of litter after he raids the box. The only solution is to get the box out of the dog's reach. Put it up on a sturdy shelf or on the dryer. Alternatively, place the box in a room that only the cat can access. Keep the door to the room closed and install a cat door. The door should be smaller than the dog can use or should be up high so only the cat can jump through. You also can use a child's gate to keep the dog out of the cat's litter box room.

LITTER BOX OUTDOORS

If you live in the country, you may prefer that your indoor-outdoor cat uses the great outdoors for his bathroom. That way you don't have to deal with a litter box at all.

Some cats don't need any training. They just prefer the outdoors. Others must be shown what you want, though. First, get a second litter box and put it outside. Leave the indoor box where it is for now. Show kitty the new box. Transfer some feces from his indoor box into the outdoor box.

Once kitty has used the outdoor box a few times, get rid of the indoor box. Now you must either let kitty out frequently or install a cat door so he can get to the box when necessary.

After a few weeks, remove the outdoor box and just sprinkle some cat litter on the ground in that spot. Eventually you can stop putting litter out and kitty will just go outside. If you have a child's sandbox in your yard, you must keep it covered to prevent the cat from defecating there. Children can be infected by parasites passed in the cat's feces.

Your cat may need an indoor box during episodes of bad weather when he doesn't want to go outdoors. Keep an eye on the weather so you are ready to supply a box when necessary. (See next section for tips about training an outdoor cat to use a box.)

LITTER BOX TRAINING AND TYPE OF LITTER

Cats have a natural instinct to use litter. Kittens learn their normal behavior, including how to use the litter box, from their mother. The easiest way to train a kitten to use the box is to leave it with its mother until it is ten to twelve weeks old. By then just about all kittens have learned proper toilet habits.

Perhaps your kitten is younger, or you just got him from the animal shelter, or he's been an outside kitty. In any case, he doesn't seem to know how to use the box. You must show him what to do.

First, realize that your house is a big space for a little kitten.

He may be all the way in the living room when he gets the urge to void, and the litter box is far away in another part of the house. Consider using two or more litter boxes if you have a large house or more than two or three cats.

Show your kitten the litter box the moment you first bring him home. Then take him there several times a day. Hold his paws and show him how to scratch in the litter. Make sure the box isn't too tall for him to enter comfortably.

Watch kitty carefully, and when he goes into a corner and begins sniffing you should take him to the box again. If you catch him in the act, just pick him up by the scruff of the neck and deposit him in the litter box.

If you find an accident after it happens, there is nothing you can do to tell kitty he was bad. He doesn't know that the pile of feces you are rubbing his nose in was the result of an action he did previously. He may "look guilty," but that is because he knows you get mad when you see feces or urine. He doesn't connect his previous action with the mess.

If you do find a pile of feces somewhere, pick it up with a paper towel and put it in the litter box. Take kitty there and let him sniff it. To prevent kitty from using the same place on the carpet repeatedly, you must remove all traces and odors of the accident. (See "Odor Control.")

Occasional mistakes happen. But it is your responsibility to prevent your cat from making mistakes in the first place. That means you need to either watch him or keep him confined.

When you can't be nearby to supervise, put the kitten in a small room with the litter box, food, and water. Once he uses his box routinely, you can let him into the rest of the house. If you have a very large house, continue to restrict the cat's access to certain rooms until you know he can find the box.

Confining also may be necessary when retraining an adult cat to use the box after mistakes have been made. However, simply confining a cat with its box is not sufficient in cases where a previously trained cat stops using the box. Once the cat gets access to the rest of the house, the bad behavior often returns.

It is essential that you also find the cause of the house soiling and correct that. (See "Defecating Out of the Litter Box" or "Urinating Outside the Box.")

What kind of litter is best? Cats are very picky about the type of litter they like. Studies show that cats prefer sand-type litter or clay litter with a fine consistency. Yet many cats use deodorized, dust-free clay litter without trouble. Other choices include wood chips, sawdust, newspaper, or alfalfa pellets.

Once you find a brand of litter that your cat likes, then don't switch brands. If you must switch, gradually blend the new with the old to help kitty adjust.

Put about two inches of litter in the box. The cat needs enough litter to cover the feces but not so much he makes a mess all over the floor.

What about training an outdoor cat to use an indoor litter box? A cat that goes outdoors can present a problem if your vet wants a stool sample, if you want to know if kitty is urinating normally, or if the cat has to stay indoors for any reason. Many people think that it is impossible to train an outdoor cat to use a litter box. Yet when an outdoor cat is boarded or kept in a veterinary hospital, he inevitably uses the litter tray without being "trained" at all. So it is possible for any cat to use a box.

You can retrain your outdoor cat to use the litter box. Consider using dirt or a sand-type litter at first to give the cat a familiar substance in which to dig.

For the first few days, confine the cat in a room with the box and his food. When he gets the urge to eliminate, he will use the box. Gradually increase the time the cat is allowed access to the rest of the house.

LOST CAT

What should you do if your cat is missing? Whether kitty is an outdoor cat or has escaped from the indoors, don't wait too long to see if she will return. Tell your neighbors that your cat is missing. Search your neighborhood by making a progressively widening spiral around your home.

Notify veterinary clinics in your area in case your cat has been injured and is receiving care. Give a complete description of your cat including her coat and eye color, age, weight, sex, and any distinguishing marks.

Stray cats may be picked up by animal control. Call your local animal control, SPCA, humane society, or other groups that take in strays. Don't rely on the animal shelter to notify you when your cat is found. Sometimes a shelter employee will incorrectly note the sex of a cat, or will describe its color differently than you do. Go to the shelter every other day to see for yourself. Call the Humane Society's Lost Pet Hotline (see appendix) to report your cat.

Make signs that describe your cat and post them in your neighborhood. But don't assume that anyone has read them. Read the "found" columns in every local newspaper.

You can prevent heartache by keeping a collar and ID tag on your cat. Both outdoor and indoor cats need identification. Even the most reliable indoor cat can become frightened and somehow escape. Thousands of cats are never recovered because their owners cannot be found. Others are hurt but are taken to veterinary hospitals by kind strangers. Their future depends on a reliable way to find their owners. Put both your phone number and that of a friend on the tag so someone can be notified if you aren't home.

Take a few "identification" photos of your cat that show her markings clearly. Views from the front and side will help show people exactly what your cat looks like. If you are careful and a bit lucky, you will never need to use them.

MEDICATING YOUR CAT

Your vet has given you pills or drops to give your cat. How will you get them down? You can try several methods until you find one that works best for you.

The method most veterinarians use is the put-it-down-the-throat technique. Hold the cat's head with your left hand (if you are right-handed). Your thumb is on the right side of the cat's upper jaw, and your fingers on the left side of the upper jaw. Tilt the cat's head up so she is looking at the ceiling. When the nose is straight up, the throat is straight down.

The next steps must be done quickly. (Practice these motions without a pill first.) Hold the pill in your right hand between your thumb and forefinger. Now use your third or fourth finger to open the cat's lower jaw. Drop the pill down into the back of the throat just as far as you can. It is important that the pill be in the center of the throat. If it lands on the side of the tongue, kitty can use her tongue to bring it back up.

Use your forefinger to push the pill down. Push the pill far back on the base of the tongue. Then close kitty's mouth and hold it there. Stroke her throat to get her to swallow. But remember, no amount of stroking the throat will work if the pill isn't centered behind the base of the tongue.

The procedure must be done quickly. Once you have kitty's mouth open, drop the pill in and push your finger down in one quick move. Your finger then gets out of the way so it doesn't

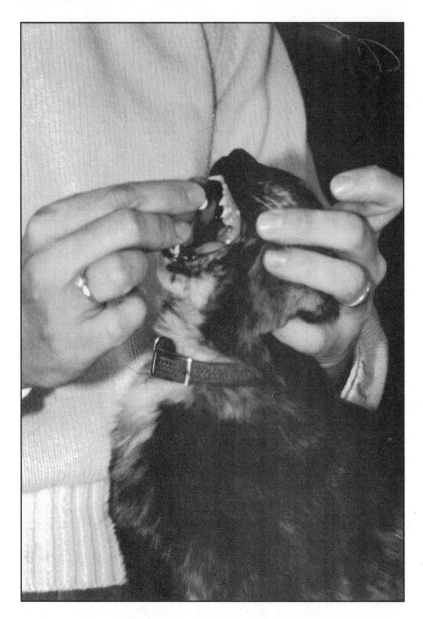

Drop a pill straight down the center of the throat.

meet kitty's teeth too soon. It happens so fast that most cats don't have time to shut their mouths voluntarily.

You can also use a "piller," an instrument that holds the pill in place of your fingers, to get the pill down your cat's throat; take care to be gentle since these can injure the back of the throat.

With a liquid medicine, you open the cat's mouth the same way and just squirt it in using your dropper or syringe. Or just lift the side of kitty's lip and squirt the liquid in there.

If kitty squirms too much, kneel on the floor. Hold your cat facing away from you between your legs. Open the mouth with one hand by squeezing at the corners of the mouth. Use your other hand to drop the pill down the throat.

Wrap your cat tightly in a towel if she reaches up to scratch you. Leave only her head protruding. Then proceed with the steps just described.

If your cat salivates a lot, it is probably because she tasted the medicine. You can avoid this problem by getting the pill down more quickly and making sure it hasn't dissolved at all before it goes down. If the cat salivates a lot with liquid medicine, use the following method.

Whether your cat is quicker than you are, or she salivates heavily, sometimes the direct technique doesn't work. What now? You can try the hide-it-in-the-food technique. What *doesn't* work is to hide a whole pill in a little piece of cheese. Kitty will just eat the cheese around the pill and leave the pill for you.

Mixing the medicine with kitty's whole bowl of canned food also won't work. If she doesn't eat it all, she will not get her full dose of medicine.

As long as your medicine is not a long-acting pill (these are coated to dissolve slowly), then you can crush the pill. Use the flat part of a butter knife to smash the pill into a powder, and then mix it with something really good and strong-tasting. Mix it in thoroughly. Use only enough food to make one or two bites at most. Give it to kitty before her meal so she is sure to eat it all. (Note: Do not mix a medicine containing tetracycline with any dairy products.)

You can mix a liquid the same way if your cat hates the liquid or foams at the mouth when it's given. Use a spoonful of something really good-tasting and mix it thoroughly with the medicine.

MEOWING TOO MUCH

Does your cat meow too much, or not at all? Certain cat breeds are stronger meowers than others. Siamese and related breeds are the most noted for being vocal. Their unusual or excessive meowing is an inherited trait.

Some cats become more vocal when they are upset. For instance, cats meow a lot after moving to a new home or changing to a new schedule. The cat will settle down with time. A consistent new schedule helps the cat adjust quickly.

Cats that suddenly meow a lot but have never done so in the past are probably sick or uncomfortable. A cat that meows while being picked up or held could be in pain. In either case, take the cat to the vet for a checkup.

Does your cat meow obnoxiously until you pick him up? If so, congratulations! You have allowed your cat to train you. Other cats meow until they are petted or fed. Their owners try and try to ignore them, but finally become exasperated and give in. The cat has learned not only to meow to get what it wants, but that the longer it meows, the better the chances of reward.

Most cats do this to some extent, but it can become a behavior problem. If your cat has become rude, you can train him to stop. Use your squirt bottle and give him a sharp spray of water when he becomes demanding. Give your cat attention only when he is quiet. Try to pick him up or feed him only when he is *not* meowing.

Does your cat meow in the middle of the night, or early in the morning, and wake you up? Do you get up and feed or pet him? If so, you are rewarding his behavior and encouraging him to continue.

Try changing kitty's feeding time to later in the day. Use your water bottle or make a loud noise to frighten kitty when he bothers you. Another trick is to hook up a hair dryer with an on-off switch next to your bed. Use an extension cord to place the hair dryer near the place kitty sits while he meows. Then turn it on when he starts meowing. That way you don't have to get up. If your cat persists, close kitty in a far-away room until you are ready to get up. A few experiences like this will keep him quiet.

MOVING TO A NEW HOME

Moving is usually a traumatic experience for cats. Because they have a strong sense of territory and home, they may have trouble adjusting to a new home. You can make things easier for your cat, though.

The weeks before moving are often chaotic. With your packing and hectic schedule, kitty knows something is going on. Try to give him lots of attention and reassurance.

Get a cat carrier well before you move. Allow your cat to get used to its presence. Make the carrier into a bed and leave the door open so your cat jumps in on his own. Make it into a toy by rubbing catnip inside. Or put his food in the carrier so he has to eat in there.

Put kitty in the carrier on moving day. The last thing you need is to have your frightened cat run away at this time. Put the carrier in the quietest spot in the house while your belongings are being removed.

Leave kitty in the carrier when you get to your new home. Then set up his food, litter box, and scratching post in one small room. Put the cat in the room, close the door, and leave him there while you unpack and arrange the furniture. This is not being cruel or isolating him. On the contrary, when a cat is insecure or frightened, he likes being in a quiet, secure, enclosed space.

Let your cat out to explore the house only after all the action has stopped and you are alone. If your cat has been an outdoor cat or has a tendency to escape through open doors, put him back in his room any time there are people coming and going. He will feel more secure knowing that he has a place all his own.

Outdoor cats should not be let outside for at least a week, preferably two. Wait until your cat seems secure in his new home. He needs time to realize this is where he belongs.

How can you prevent your cat from trying to return to your old home? The older your cat and the longer you lived in your old home, the more likely the cat is to want to return. If the old home is nearby, then you are almost guaranteed to have problems if you let your cat outside. If that is the case, keep your cat inside for a long time (up to a month), and even consider making him an indoor cat. Take some feces from the litter box and put them in your new yard before you let your cat out, to "mark" it as his.

Some cats stop eating or meow continually right after a move. It's okay to "spoil" your cat a bit if this is the case. Give him lots of attention and tempt him with tasty treats. Distract him with toys and tease him into playing. But don't let him manipulate you into allowing bad behavior. Consistency on your part will do the most for making him feel secure. The sooner you can set up a regular schedule of work, play, and feeding, the sooner your cat will feel secure again.

OBESITY

How can you get your fat, lazy cat to slim down and perk up? Obesity is becoming a big problem in the modern cat. We take such good care of our cats, and provide them with such optimal nutrition, that frequently they are overweight. Fat cats aren't just cute. They are prone to urinary tract blockage, diabetes, and other health problems.

Weigh yourself, plus and minus your cat, on the bathroom scale. Record the weight once a month to keep track. Many cats, like people, gain weight in the winter and lose it in the summer. That is because cold weather stimulates the appetite.

What is the best weight for a cat? That partly depends on his body size. Don't fool yourself, though, by insisting that your cat is "big-boned" when he's not. Roll kitty over and inspect his belly. Does it jiggle? When kitty is standing, is there a lump hanging down between his rear legs?

Ask your vet to evaluate your cat's weight at your next visit. The vet will weigh your cat, give you an idea of his ideal weight, and suggest a diet food.

There are many diet or "light" cat foods available, so if your cat won't eat one you can try another. Make the switch gradually to be sure your cat continues to eat. (See "Feeding Changes and New Diets.") Cats cannot go on crash diets. To remain healthy, they must lose weight slowly yet continue to eat well. Set a goal of one pound of weight loss per month.

Obesity is caused by lack of exercise and too much food.

One note of caution: If your overweight cat stops eating, take him to the vet at once. Fat cats are prone to liver disease (hepatic lipidosis) when they don't eat for several days.

If you have one cat, the dieting process is easy. You just measure out the day's ration and that's that. Those of you who own several cats have a bigger problem. If you are really dedicated, you will feed each cat separately. For many people though, that isn't an option.

The next best choice is to feed diet food to all your cats. As long as they are all over one year old and your vet gives the go-ahead, they can all eat the diet food even if they aren't all overweight. If you have one younger cat and several older fat cats, consider feeding the younger cat a bit extra on the side, leaving the diet food out the rest of the time.

Diet food is available in both canned and dry varieties. Don't sabotage your cat's diet by adding ordinary canned food to his diet dry food. And avoid treats that add calories. Remember, those boxes of little cat treats you buy in the store aren't calorie-free. And your cat is very small compared to you, so what may be a "little treat" in your eyes can add a lot of calories to the cat.

Obesity is caused by an imbalance between calories taken in and calories expended. You can approach a diet from both aspects: reducing kitty's intake and increasing his exercise. Exercise is important for every cat's health and well-being.

Consider getting another cat to play with Chubby. Set aside a play time for your cat every day. Make or buy some toys to stimulate his mind and body. Perhaps he's forgotten how much fun playing can be, so you must remind him.

ODOR CONTROL

Odor left from house soiling and odors in the litter box are the biggest odor problems for cat owners. Tomcat urine has the strongest odor, but female cats' urine also smells bad. What's more, odor in your carpet can perpetuate the cat's house soiling habits.

See "Litter Box Mess and Smell" for tips on reducing that odor. For problems in the rest of the house, get products that are specifically made to neutralize urine odor. These can be purchased at your veterinarian's office or pet store. Be sure that the product you are using is an odor neutralizer and not just a deodorant. Don't use any cleaner that contains ammonia, since urine also contains ammonia and the smell may still attract the cat.

Several miscellaneous products also work well to eliminate urine odor. Try one of these if you cannot find a specific urine odor neutralizer.

- Vinegar
- Woolite Spray Foam Rug Cleaner
- Scope Mouthwash

First, blot up all the urine you can with a towel. Then soak the area thoroughly with your neutralizer. Remember that the urine probably soaked all the way through your carpet and into the pad. Your cleaner must do the same. Let it soak for a while, then blot up the excess. You may need to repeat the process on stubborn odors. Always test a small carpet patch first for color-fastness.

Professional carpet cleaning may be necessary for widespread problems. Question the company about their pet-odor approach. Be sure they use an odor neutralizer made for pet urine.

OFF-LIMITS FURNITURE, COUNTERTOPS, AND ROOMS

"I can't seem to train Sheeba not to get on the kitchen counter," the woman complained. "I put her down every time I catch her there, but she just gets back up again when I turn my back."

Sheeba wasn't suffering any adverse consequences for her actions, so she continued the bad behavior. Does your cat do the same thing? It is not enough to lift your cat gently off the counter and put her on the floor. You must make the act of getting on the counter an unpleasant experience. Use a loud horn or squirt bottle to get kitty off the counter the instant you notice her there. Be quick and consistent. Your reaction must be *instantaneous* for best results. If your water bottle isn't within reach, clap your hands and hiss loudly.

It is difficult to keep a cat off the counter or other furniture when you are not there. One alternative is to close the door to the kitchen. Another choice is to set "booby traps" to give kitty a scare when she jumps up in your absence.

Be careful that you don't set up anything that could harm your cat. Some people use mousetraps, but set them upside-down so kitty's paw can't become trapped. Others make a pile of empty soda cans that topple loudly when disturbed. Double-sided cellophane tape laid on the counter also may work. Or lay sheets of aluminum foil on the counter—cats hate the cold, slippery, and noisy surface. Some cats are afraid of balloons and will be deterred by balloons taped to the counter.

No matter how well your cat seems to be trained, you still must assume that she may get up on the counter when you aren't home. So you should never leave anything out that could harm her if she were to eat or play with it. Also consider that if you never leave food out, then your cat won't have any great desire to get on the counter. Leaving food out gives kitty a "reward" for jumping there when you aren't looking.

You also can train your cat not to enter certain rooms of your house, be it your bedroom, your office, or another room you would like to keep clear of cat hair.

First, resolve never to let your cat in that room again. No exceptions. Keep the door to that room closed unless you are there to defend it. Otherwise kitty will be able to go in the room without consequence.

Then consider how cats defend their own territory against other cats: They hiss and growl and chase the intruder away. You will do the same thing.

When kitty approaches the room, jump up, clap your hands, and hiss. As soon as he backs away, relax and sit down again. Keep your behavior toward your cat perfectly normal in all other respects. Don't apologize or make a big deal out of it.

You also can use a squirt water bottle, loud horn, or other device to deter your cat from going into the room. Motion-detector alarms work as long as you don't go in the room either. The alarm sound must be loud enough to scare the cat but should be short and self-limiting.

Your cat won't take long to get the message. Eventually you won't have to keep the door closed at all. The only exception to this is when the cat is not allowed to sleep in the bedroom, since you can't tell your cat to go away when you are asleep. (See "Sleeping" for more tips.)

What about allowing your cat in some rooms, some of the time? Don't expect kitty to understand this concept. If the room's door is usually kept closed, put a cat door in the door of the room. You can close off the cat door when necessary. Your cat will learn to test the cat door to find out when it is "open." Alternatively, just close the room's door when the room is off limits. Leave it open when kitty may enter.

OLD AGE: CAT CARE

The thin gray tabby peered out at me from her carrier. At her age, a trip to the vet was nothing new. She calmly allowed me to take her from the box. Then the cat crouched on the exam table and quietly endured my probing hands.

"She's just not right," Aster's owner said. "I know that older cats slow down some, but all she does is sleep. And her appetite isn't very good anymore. Is this normal for her age or should I be worried?"

I completed my physical exam without finding anything remarkable. Still, I explained, "Older cats often have medical problems that we can't find with just a physical exam. We need to take blood and urine samples to find Aster's problem. Chances are that we can help Aster feel better, once we know what's going on internally."

What are the "normal" changes that occur with age? Older cats will naturally slow down and lose body tone. Some cats suffer from gradual loss of hearing or sight. Others develop arthritis in one or more joints. Your cat may become more dependent, asking for extra attention or preferring to stay near you.

The average life span of a cat is around twelve to fifteen years. But since many cats succumb to disease or injury, that is not the cat's potential life span. Many cats live into their late teens in good health. Twenty is considered very old. The oldest cats on record lived to their thirties. Neutered cats live an average of three to five years longer than those left sexually intact.

You can help make your elderly cat's life easier. Older cats are less able to defend themselves or to see or hear approaching danger. They should be kept safely indoors.

Older cats aren't as mobile as young cats and may have trouble getting up stairs or around obstacles. Make sure your cat's food, water, and litter box are easily accessible.

Your elderly cat may not groom herself as rigorously as she did when she was younger. Brush or comb the coat daily to keep mats from developing and to help you spot any skin problems early.

Good nutrition will keep your older cat feeling young. Older cats need to eat just enough of a balanced diet to keep them from becoming over- or underweight. Stick to good-quality, name-brand foods. Some diets are specially made for geriatric cats. There are also prescription diets made for cats with specific diseases that are common in old age. These diets contain the ideal balance of nutrients your cat needs. Ask your veterinarian for advice on a specific brand or type of food for your cat.

As a cat ages, her immune system doesn't function as well as before. Your cat may be more susceptible to respiratory disease and other infections. It is just as important to continue your cat's yearly vaccinations as it was during the younger years.

Like the rest of your cat's body, her teeth wear with age too. Regular dental care is necessary for elderly cats. Your cat may not show obvious discomfort from her decayed teeth, but cats usually don't complain when they have to endure chronic pain. You may be surprised at kitty's change in attitude once those rotten old teeth are cleaned or pulled.

If your cat needs her teeth cleaned, rest assured that today's safe gas anesthetics allow us to anesthetize most older cats with minimal risk. Preoperative blood testing will reveal any potential problems so your vet can be prepared.

How can you tell whether your cat is simply slowing down due to old age, or whether she has a health problem that needs treatment? Simply put, you often can't tell. It's likely that you already watch your cat for signs of illness. You also should weigh your cat once a month to catch any weight gain or loss before it becomes severe. (Weigh yourself, plus and minus kitty, on the bathroom scale.) Yet disease may creep in slowly without definite signs.

Don't just assume that since your cat is in her teens, that her weight loss, irritability, lack of appetite, or slowing down are "normal for her age." Have your vet take a look! For instance, an older cat that forgets to use the litter box isn't necessarily becoming senile. Instead, the cat could be ill.

Many, many diseases of older cats are treatable. Still other diseases can be managed with a change in diet. Your older cat can be much more comfortable if you tend to her health.

Older cats are susceptible to failing kidneys, overactive thyroid glands, diabetes, and dental disease. Many diseases have similar signs, so even when a cat is ill it is impossible to diagnose the disease with a physical exam alone.

Veterinarians recommend yearly blood tests for all cats over ten years of age. Testing *before* a cat looks sick allows us to diagnose disease early, when the chances of successful treatment are greater. Often a change in diet can hold disease signs at bay. Although most of these diseases never go away completely, all are treatable to some extent.

Watch your older cat for:

- Weight gain or loss
- Increased thirst
- Increased urination, or not using the box
- Lumps or sores on the skin
- Discharge from the eyes or nose
- Coughing; wheezy or labored breathing
- Decreased *or* increased appetite

OLD AGE: SAYING GOOD-BYE

When is it time to let go of your cat and say good-bye? We all hope that our cats will live full lives and then pass away quietly in their sleep without suffering. Yet that doesn't occur often. Chances are that eventually you will be faced with deciding whether to have your cat put to sleep.

The decision to euthanize your cat can leave you overcome with uncertainty and guilt. Part of the emotional difficulty in deciding about euthanasia is wondering whether the time is right. Many people feel forced to make a decision about euthanasia when they don't have enough information to make that decision. You can't decide if you don't know what is wrong with your cat.

Because we provide our cats with excellent nutrition and advanced health care, they live longer and encounter many of the same chronic illnesses that people do. Diabetes, kidney disease, cancer, and heart failure all occur in cats. Yet it is important to remember that old age is not a disease. Although all cats will die eventually, many of the ailments that afflict older cats can be managed for a time.

No matter what your cat's specific problem, manage the situation in the same way. Gather as much information as possible before you make any decisions. Coping with a pet's life-threatening illness is always difficult. You will be full of questions and concerns: Is my cat suffering? Is he going to die? How am I going to pay the bills? Will I be able to provide adequate nursing care at home if my cat recovers?

At first, your emotions can be so overwhelming that you may have difficulty assessing the situation. Perhaps your cat has a severe disease that hit suddenly, requiring an emergency trip to the veterinary hospital. In other situations, your cat doesn't look too bad: Animals with kidney disease or heart failure can have such a slow onset of symptoms that you may not have noticed the problem until recently.

Don't allow yourself to feel rushed into any decision. You may have a few hours or even days to learn more about your cat's illness, to prepare yourself and your family for the possibility of your cat's death, and to make informed decisions. Make a list of your questions to bring with you to your veterinarian.

Key Questions to Ask

- What must be done immediately to save my cat's life and make him more comfortable?
- What further testing must be done to diagnose my cat's specific problem?
- What is the estimated cost of immediate care and the diagnostic workup?
- Is there a chance that my cat will need intensive care and hospitalization for an extended period of time? What will this treatment cost?
- What is the short-term prognosis for my cat's recovery? The long-term prognosis?
- What quality of life should be expected for my cat?
- Will my cat require lifelong medications or a special diet? Am I capable of ensuring that these are given? What is the long-term cost of managing my cat's illness?
- What signs will my cat show when his condition is worsening?
- How will I know when it is time to put my cat to sleep?

Often a series of diagnostic tests are necessary to determine the precise problem. Why pay for tests on an old cat that is going to die anyway? First, because he might *not* die from this problem—some diseases *are* manageable. Second, if your cat does have an incurable disease, you can avoid having him suffer needlessly. Instead of simply waiting to see if your cat gets worse, you can find out what's wrong as soon as possible. Either way you will feel at peace with your decision.

Blood tests, X rays, or even surgery may be necessary to pinpoint a diagnosis. If you have any question about your vet's diagnosis, then don't hesitate to ask for a second opinion. Your vet may send X rays to a specialist, telephone a veterinary teaching hospital, or send your cat and a copy of his records to a specialist in your area.

Ask about treatment options for your cat and the implications of each one. Consider cost, quality of life, chances of success, and your personal commitment to caring for the cat at home.

No one wants to put a price tag on their cat's life, yet cost of care is a very real consideration. It's best to be honest about your budget and ability to take on a large veterinary bill. Get a cost estimate as soon as possible, both for immediate work and for long-term care.

Ask your veterinarian for a realistic life expectancy for your cat. While no one can tell you exactly how your cat's illness will progress, you can get percentages or statistical information about other cats with similar diseases.

Your cat may require medication for the rest of his life. Very small doses often can be given in liquid form, but you might be faced with giving a pill or even injections. You may surprise yourself: Many needle-shy people have mastered the art of giving injections! Be sure to spend as much time as necessary with your veterinarian or technician until you have mastered the art of administering medications. Follow the instructions precisely and don't be afraid to ask questions.

Some diseases, such as diabetes, require a precise schedule of medications and feeding that will affect your own life significantly. Cats with other chronic diseases may need a special prescription diet. Be honest with yourself and your family: Can you stick with the program, eliminating all those scraps or treats you used to give? Your cat's health will depend on it.

Decision making and judgments are not limited to the first

time your cat's problem is diagnosed. You will ask yourself continually if your cat is suffering, if his quality of life is worthwhile, and whether you're able to contend with the continuous schedule of medications and diet. These questions should be discussed frequently with your family and veterinarian.

One of the curses and blessings we have is the ability to put our cats out of their misery. Only you can decide when the appropriate time has come. Expect your veterinarian to assist in your decision, but not to make it for you. Keep asking questions and talk openly with your family and veterinarian. By doing so you will be ready for any difficult decisions you must face.

OUTDOOR CATS AND THE CAT DOOR

Indoor-outdoor cats often drive their owners nuts with their constant meowing to go in or out. The best solution is to install a cat door. Several different types are available. Shop around for one that best suits your needs. You can install a cat door in any wood door, in a wall, or in a screen door. The cat door will allow in a bit of a cold draft, so consider that when choosing its location.

Cat doors have a plastic or rubber flap that swings aside when the cat pushes on that part. Most cat doors have some sort of locking mechanism or board that allows you to close them off when needed.

You may decide to install cat doors on one or more of your inside doors too. That way you can control your cat's access to different rooms at different times. Cat doors also allow the cat to go into rooms where the dog isn't allowed. Use a door that is smaller than your dog but big enough for your cat. Or place the

Cat doors can be installed just about anywhere.
(Photo courtesy of Borwick Innovations)

cat door high up so the dog can't get through. Place a table or shelf nearby to assist kitty's access.

One problem with cat doors is that neighbor cats learn to use them and enter your house. Wild animals have been known to enter homes via cat doors too. Some wild animals can be deterred by placing the opening of the cat door high up, so the cat can jump through but other animals might not. Another solution is to use the type of door that opens only when a cat with a certain type of collar approaches.

If you have dogs, place the cat door so it opens into the dog's yard. Your dogs will allow your cats in, but not strange cats or wild animals. You can use a large dog-size door for both the cats and dogs.

How can you train your cat to use the cat door? Let's say you have installed the cat door and now kitty is meowing at the other side of the house, asking you to let him in through the side door. That gets us to step one: Never, ever let your cat in the house by another route while you are training him to use the cat door.

Get a good-tasting treat, stick your hand out the cat door, and call. When kitty approaches, hold up the flap and allow him to enter, then give him the treat.

You will have to hold open the flap the first few times so kitty learns that this is the way to go in and out. Each time hold the flap lower, so kitty has to duck and push just a little to get through.

After a few days, put kitty's food away and let him get hungry for a few hours. Then get an extra-delectable treat—a spoonful of tuna or ice cream—and hold it out through the door. As soon as kitty smells it, let the flap down and hold the treat just inside the door. It won't be long before he finds a way to get through.

OUTDOOR CATS CONVERTED TO INDOOR CATS

Outdoors may be a risky place for your cat. An outdoor cat is exposed to cars, dogs, and other cats carrying all sorts of diseases. It is a fact that cats let outdoors live much shorter lives than those kept inside. Perhaps you have decided that your outdoor cat would be safer kept indoors.

Imagine you have recently moved from the country to the city. You wonder, "How will my cat adjust? He's so used to having acres of land to play on, and lots of mice to catch. Will he ever learn to stay inside?"

Or imagine that you own a single cat that has just been diagnosed with feline leukemia virus. The cat isn't very sick, so you want to treat him and keep him at home. But the vet has given strict instructions to never let the cat outside again. Will it be possible?

Whether the new indoor rules are due to a move or to quarantine, the adjustment can be difficult. It is possible, though, if you are patient and persistent.

There is no "gradual" way to teach a cat to stay indoors. The decision, once made, must be enforced without exception. You can make it easier on your cat by providing distractions that keep his mind off the outdoors.

Buy or make a big cat tree—the taller the better, with lots of perches. Get more than one tree for variety, and put them in different rooms of the house.

Get some cat toys and set up entertainment for your cat. Rub catnip on the toys and the cat tree. Hang a toy from a chair or table so it swings invitingly. Devote a few minutes several times a day to playing with your cat.

Leave the radio on when you are gone to provide background music for your cat. Experiment to see which types of music he likes best.

Cats like to look out windows, so be sure yours has a perch

Outdoor cats can learn to live indoors.

where he can enjoy a view. If you don't have any furniture near a window, get a commercially made cat window perch that attaches to the windowsill.

Consider building an enclosed outdoor cat run or enclosed porch for your cat. Access to the run via a cat door allows kitty to come and go as he pleases.

Your cat may try to escape out the door when it is opened. To avoid accidental escape, train him to keep away from the door. Keep a water bottle next to the door. Use it to prevent kitty from coming anywhere near the door when you are coming or going. A sharp blast of water will teach your cat to keep his distance.

What if you have a dog that uses a dog door, and your cat escapes there? One solution is to use the type of door that opens only when an animal with a special collar approaches. The other choice is to close off the room with the dog door so your cat can't get to the dog door. Your dog can come in and out from "his room." (The laundry room, garage, porch, or basement work well.) Then just let your dog in to the rest of the home when you want him to join you.

Outdoor cats must sometimes be retrained to use a litter box. Most cats learn to do so without difficulty. (See "Litter Box Training and Type of Litter.")

Finally, steel yourself for a few weeks of meowing, complaining, and beseeching looks. When kitty asks to go outside, distract him with a game or petting. Eventually your cat will adjust to being inside.

OUTDOOR CATS: RISKS AND BENEFITS

Cats love playing outside. Yet the outdoors carries many dangers to cats. City cats should never be allowed outdoors. The risks are far too great. Cats get run over by cars, pick up deadly diseases from other cats, and acquire fight wounds that cause your veterinary bills to soar.

Outdoor cats are most appropriate in the country, where they can help control mice and gophers. Cats enjoy catching grasshoppers and climbing trees. With a cat door installed, kitty can come and go as she pleases. Many cats fare well outdoors in the country. But you must acknowledge the risks involved.

Be sure your cat has a collar and identification tag so you can be notified if she is found hurt somewhere. All outdoor cats should have a collar, even if you live far in the country and you are sure your cat never wanders off. You never know when your cat may be chased off by another animal and end up far from home.

What about a kitten's first trip to the great outdoors? The kitten should have all her vaccinations, including boosters, before she is allowed out. Kittens should be supervised outdoors until they are self-sufficient (at least five or six months old), know their way around, and can find shelter. When you go indoors, take the kitten in with you.

There is no way to train a cat to behave outside; once you decide to let yours out, she is on her own for better or worse. Your cat may be well trained and quiet, but you can't control her reactions to birds, dogs, other cats, and scary noises such as the neighbor's lawn mower. The only sure way to prevent a cat from getting lost, running away, or going into the street is to keep her on a leash or indoors.

Perhaps you have wondered whether your cat can be trained to stay in the yard, thus staying out of harm's way. Some cats just naturally seem to stay in their own yards, never wandering far. Yet sometimes even these cats wander off out of curiosity or are scared away by a passing dog. Don't count on your cat staying near home once you let her out. (See "Moving to a New Home" for tips on keeping your cat nearby after you move.)

What if your cat gets "stuck" up a tree? Only in rare instances is the cat really "stuck." A cat can come down what she climbed up, but she is certain not to do so while you are waiting beneath. Go away and see what happens. Leave some food at the base of the tree.

Take the responsibility of caring for your outdoor cat should she become injured or ill. Keep your cat's vaccinations up-to-date. Expect more frequent vet visits, watch your cat closely for signs of illness, and be ready for the inevitable day when kitty doesn't come home.

Perhaps you have decided to keep your cat indoors after all. See "Indoor Cats" for information about indoor cats.

PAIN RELIEF

Imagine you accidentally stepped on kitty's tail. Now you feel terrible—her tail is obviously sore. Even though you plan to take her to the veterinarian tomorrow, you would like to give her a little something for the pain right now. What should you use?

The best and safest pain treatment is the use of heat or cold. For acute (recent) injuries, use a cold pack to reduce swelling and relieve pain. Applying cold gives as much pain relief as many drugs.

Chronic injuries respond better to heat. For instance, an abscess that is slowly healing will heal better if you apply a hot compress for ten minutes two to three times daily.

Be careful if you are considering using a heating pad for kitty. Cats that can't get up and move around have become severely burned just from lying on a heating pad. If you use one, cover it with lots of towels and check kitty every few hours. Hot water bottles are safer.

What about pain-relieving drugs? Unfortunately, the pills you take for your own aches and pains can be deadly to your cat. One acetaminophen pill (Tylenol, for example) can kill a cat. Aspirin and ibuprofin (Advil, Motrin) also can make your cat very sick.

Why the problems? Cats don't have the enzymes in their livers that most other animals have. So cats don't break down drugs in the same way that people or dogs do. Aspirin is the only pain reliever that veterinarians prescribe for cats, and even that must be given at a very low dose at long intervals. (A cat takes at least two days to metabolize aspirin.) So you *cannot* assume that your ten-pound cat gets one-tenth the dose of a one-hundred-pound human. Both the amount and the timing of the dose are very different.

If you think your cat is in pain, call your vet to get advice about what to do. Use heat or cold for minor problems or until you can reach your vet.

PLANTS

Some cats love to dig in the dirt of potted plants. Others enjoy munching on greenery. If your cat has either of these habits, or just destroys your plants as a form of entertainment, then you will have to train her to keep away from the plants.

Your cat will not be trained instantly. That means you must put any poisonous plants out of kitty's reach. Cats are most likely to get into plants that are at floor level or on low tables. They are less likely to get into plants that are up on shelves. Hanging plants is the best way to keep them out of the cat's reach.

Your cat must be trained both when you are home and when you are away. If you are not there to supervise, you should either put kitty in a room where she can't get to the plants or put something in or on the plants as a deterrent.

Cats that dig in potting soil can be deterred by covering the dirt with waxed paper or foil. (Poke some holes in it to allow air circulation.) Other choices: Lay chicken wire over the soil; pile wood chips on top of the dirt; or put a layer of stones on the dirt. Some people place a mousetrap upside down in the pot. That way it is triggered when the cat steps nearby but it doesn't catch the cat's paw. You also can combine two techniques by placing a mousetrap under some foil.

If your cat is a plant-chewer, spray a bad-tasting substance on the leaves. Use Bitter Apple spray (available at most pet stores) or hot pepper sauce.

When your cat approaches a plant, use a squirt water bottle or a loud horn to scare her away. Keep your squirt bottle in easy reach so you can act quickly when kitty misbehaves. If you can't grab the water bottle in time, jump up, hiss, and clap your hands to get kitty away from the plant.

A plant-chewing habit is more than an annoyance. Your safest course is to train your cat not to chew on any plants at all

Cats must be trained to stay away from plants.

and to keep plants out of reach. Though we can't give a complete list here, some common poisonous houseplants include:

azalea	Jerusalem cherry
dieffenbachia	mistletoe
Easter lily	nightshade
English ivy	oleander
holly	philodendron
Japanese yew	tiger lily

If your cat chews on or eats any plant, you should call your veterinarian's office. They can look up the plant in question and tell you whether it is poisonous or not. Another good source of information is the National Animal Poison Control Center. (See appendix for contact information.)

Cats have a natural desire to chew on plants. What plants are safe? Catnip or ordinary grass can be grown in flat trays for your cat's enjoyment. You can get seeds and growing kits at some pet stores. Plant several dishes and rotate them as one gets chewed down. Your cat can learn that your good plants are "off limits" while it is acceptable to chew on her special grass.

PLAYING AND TOYS

Playing with your cat is just as much fun for you as it is for kitty. Chances are you bought your share of cat toys from the supermarket and pet store. Yet some of those toys go ignored while kitty remains entranced with your shoelaces. What makes the best toy for your cat?

Cat toys must be both safe and fun. When shopping for cat

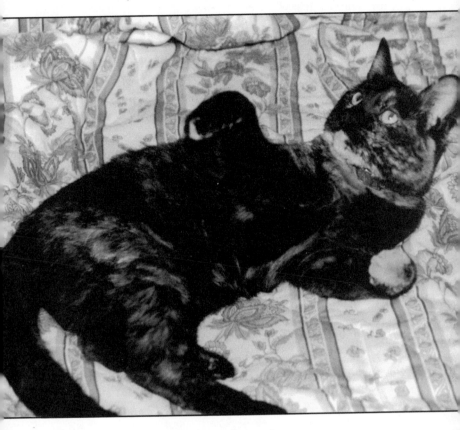

Play is good exercise.

toys, consider entertainment value, safety, and quality. Assume that any small parts will detach and could be swallowed. Your best bets are catnip-filled fabric mice, one- to two-inch balls, or "fishing pole" type toys that have something that dangles and jumps on a string that is attached to a pole.

You don't have to buy specially made playthings, though. Consider these inexpensive alternatives:

- Empty paper bag
- Wadded-up paper balls
- Tennis, Ping-Pong, or racquet balls
- Empty cardboard box with a hole cut in it
- Small lightweight rug on a slick floor
- Your children's discarded stuffed toys
- Empty tissue box with a ball inside

Some cats like to play on a slick linoleum floor when there is a small, lightweight throw rug to "ski" on. Put kitty's favorite toy under the rug and move it around so she tunnels under the rug to get it.

Cats like variation in their playthings. Change the toys once a week so kitty won't be bored. Put extra toys in the closet, then bring one out when it is time to play.

Certain toys can be dangerous and should be avoided. Don't let kitty play with string, since it could be swallowed accidentally. Instead, try larger items, such as shoelaces or rope, and put them away when you are not there to supervise. Avoid any toy that is small enough to fit in the cat's mouth or that has small pieces that could come apart.

Wrestling with kitty seems like fun—at first. But it is best to never use your hands and arms to play with your cat. Kitty doesn't know when a bite or scratch is too hard. When you feel a pinch, you may instinctively swat back, but kitty thinks you're still playing and doesn't know when to stop. Wrestling in fun also can teach a cat that it is okay to pounce on people.

So, resist your first impulse and reserve your hands for petting. When kitty wants to play, get out a toy and direct her attention toward that.

Some people insist their cats don't like to play. "My cat is all grown up," they say, "and she doesn't play anymore. That sort of thing is for kittens. But my cat is getting a little pudgy. How can I get her to exercise?"

It's a myth that cats always stop their playing behavior with age. But some cats do get fat and lazy, and it is up to you to stimulate them to play and work off those extra calories.

Cats that sit around all the time just might be bored. "Ho-hum, just another day of sitting around," thinks kitty as she watches you make breakfast and get ready for work. Give kitty a pleasant surprise and entice her to play for a bit. Bring home some catnip to get her in the mood, then attach a toy to a string and run through the house.

Play peek-a-boo around the couch, make your toes act like a mouse under your bed covers, or throw a paper ball for kitty. Try a game of hide-and-seek for some real fun. You have to give away your position a bit at first so kitty will understand the game; just peek around a corner, then duck out of sight, then peek out again. Kitty will look at you like you're nuts at first, but she is likely to join in the fun. Isn't that what cats are for?

SCRATCHING FURNITURE

Sharpening her claws is part of a cat's normal behavior. Scratching also serves to leave the cat's scent. Cats scratch when playing or stretching too.

You can't take away that behavior, but you can redirect it to prevent your cat from ruining all your furniture. You must be

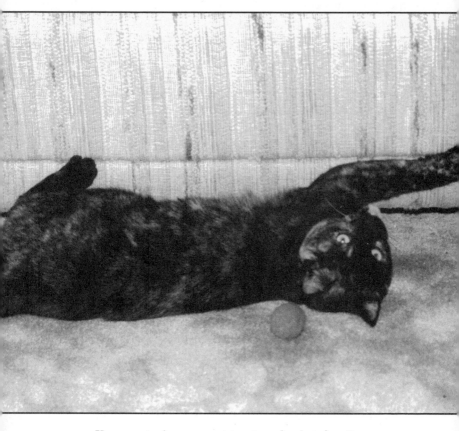

You can train your cat to stop clawing furniture.

consistent and patient. It takes time for kitty to learn what you want. The longer a cat has used a particular object as her scratching post, the longer it may take to train her to use something else. But don't give up, because it is possible. For tips on scratching and biting people, see "Biting, Scratching, and Clawing People."

Some people allow their cat to scratch their old, worn furniture. But when they eventually get new furniture, training the cat to use a scratching post will be more difficult. Start training your cat to use a post today.

Protect furniture surfaces by covering them with foil or plastic wrap that you tack firmly in place. Apply this protective barrier onto the corners of couches and chairs where kitty scratches most.

Try one of the cat-repellent sprays available at pet stores. These have an odor that is offensive to cats and may prevent your cat from harming the furniture.

Consider using furniture shampoo to clean your cat's favorite scratching spots. Since the cat's scratching serves to leave her scent, cleaning the furniture will remove that scent and may help make it less attractive.

None of these deterrents will work all the time. You cannot train your cat when you are not home. During the training period, confine kitty to one room while you are away. Consider this a short-term method of speeding up the training process. The less you allow your cat to do the bad behavior, the quicker she will learn what you want.

Now find something for your cat to use as a scratching post. Without doing this, your training is doomed to failure. Cats cannot resist sharpening their claws. They will become very frustrated if punished for using the furniture but given no alternative.

You can buy or make a traditional post with carpet firmly tacked onto a piece of wood. You also can use tubular cardboard cement forms ("Sonotubes"—at masonry or construction stores) for the frame instead of wood. Or get a medium-size log, complete with bark, for kitty. There are also commercially made cardboard scratching boxes.

A cat tree may be more appealing than a simple small post. Trees have several platforms and boxes that can extend all the way to the ceiling. An elaborate tree or condo offers the combination of scratching post, hiding place, and bed that is hard to resist.

Whatever you choose, make it appealing and easy to use. The scratching surface should be at least one foot long (better yet, two to three feet), so kitty can extend her legs to scratch. A vertical post must have a wide sturdy base since your cat won't use something that wobbles. Consider getting more than one so kitty doesn't have to go far to find a place to sharpen her claws. Get some catnip and rub it all over the post.

Now be sure you have water bottles, loud whistles, or horns strategically placed throughout the house. When kitty begins to scratch the furniture, make her stop immediately by squirting her or making a loud noise. Then pick her up and take her to the scratching post. Pick up her front feet and rub them on the post. Give her lots of praise. If you follow this routine consistently, your cat will be trained in a short time.

If you seem to be having trouble getting through to your cat, the location or the type of post may not be to kitty's liking. Is the post sturdy, or does it teeter under the cat's weight? Is it long enough for your cat to stretch out fully while scratching?

Try to get a post with a texture similar to the piece of furniture your cat likes best. Move the piece of furniture and put the post there instead. Or cover the furniture with plastic and place the post directly in front of it. Once kitty uses the post, gradually move it to the location you want it to stay.

Kittens may scratch and claw at drapes when playing. This play behavior has different motivation from scratching furniture. Use a spray bottle or loud horn to stop your cat when you catch her in the act. Then give her a toy to show her what she can do instead.

SHEDDING EXCESSIVELY: HAIRBALLS

Shedding is a normal event for all cats. Hair growth increases each summer and decreases each winter. Longer daylight hours and higher temperatures stimulate shedding each spring. However, cats kept in a warm and well-lit house may shed year-round because their bodies don't "know" that the seasons have changed. Short of turning out the lights and turning off the heat, there are some things you can do to ease the situation.

Regular brushing will remove some of the cat's hair before it is shed onto your belongings. Wipe your cat with a wet towel before brushing to reduce fly-away hair. Brush your cat every day when shedding is severe.

An occasional shampoo, especially during heavy shedding seasons, also helps remove excess hair. Brush before and after bathing. Give long-haired cats a "lion's cut" each spring to keep them cool and get rid of hair. (See "Grooming Basics.")

Use a hand vacuum to touch up in between vacuuming the whole house. Run a humidifier in your home to reduce fly-away hair. Keep lint brushes handy to brush off your clothes and furniture. Avoid wearing velvet and corduroy, or any color of clothes that clashes with your cat's coat color.

Cats shed more when they are nervous. The hair that falls out is hair that was ready to shed, but does so all at once. When a cat is frightened, she "fluffs up" her coat. This is done by tensing the little muscles around the hair shafts. If the hair was about ready to shed, it is more likely to do so when that happens.

A poor diet can lead to a dull coat and increased shedding. To help keep the coat healthy, feed your cat the best-quality food possible.

Profuse shedding may be due to skin disease or sign of a bigger problem. Look closely at your cat's coat to detect any blemishes. Is her coat shiny and full? Are there any thin spots, signs of irritation, or broken hairs? Does your cat scratch or groom herself excessively? Fleas, ringworm, allergies, or hormonal imbalances may cause changes in the hair coat. (See "Hair Loss" and "Itching.")

Any illness that affects the cat's entire body may cause a change in her coat too. A veterinary exam will help determine whether your cat is sick or just shedding normally.

Hairballs are the result of the cat ingesting too much hair. The problem occurs in long-haired cats year round and in short-haired cats during shedding season. Some cats vomit hairballs, which are actually a mixture of hair and food. You might hear a "hairball cough" that sounds as if the cat is trying to get something out of her throat. (See "Vomiting, Bulimia, Hairballs.")

The most important way to prevent hairballs is to brush your cat regularly. Using a hairball remedy helps, but it doesn't prevent your cat from eating hair in the first place.

Hairball remedies are laxatives that come in several flavors and brands. All are some form of flavored petroleum jelly. You also can use unflavored petroleum jelly. Don't use oils or digestible fats. There is a risk that the cat could aspirate (breathe in) any oil. What's more, digestible fats or oils have no laxative effect.

Follow label instructions carefully. Don't use a hairball remedy on your cat every day, except for the first few days you are treating the problem. Daily use of any laxative can interfere with the cat's nutrition. Use the hairball remedy weekly during the shedding season.

SHY, TIMID, OR FEARFUL CATS

Does your cat run and hide when your friends visit? Is he sensitive to seemingly small changes in your home? Or is he unusually afraid of thunderstorms or other loud noises? Timid cats may behave lovingly with their owners but become irrationally fearful when anything unusual occurs.

Most shy cats don't need any special treatment. You can make adjustments in your lifestyle to avoid creating stress for your cat. However, if you would like your cat's behavior to improve, you can try a process called *desensitization* to help your cat overcome his fears. Sometimes antianxiety drugs also are used for the short term to help cats overcome extreme fear. With desensitization, the cat is gradually exposed to the things he fears until he becomes accustomed to them.

For instance, if your cat is uncomfortable with strangers, invite friends over for a few "practice" visits. Choose people with quiet body language, low voices, and a calm demeanor. If you have exuberant friends, meet them elsewhere. Invite just a few people at first, not a big party.

Allow your cat a "hiding place," a room where the guests don't go. But don't let him outside, or he will just escape and won't learn anything. At first, ask your guests to ignore the cat totally. After a few quiet visits, your cat may decide to peek out of his hiding place to see what's going on.

If your cat eats meals, ask one of your guests to feed the cat. Put the food in a room where the cat can see and hear your guests, but where he feels safe enough to eat. Gradually move the food bowl closer to your guests over several different visits.

Another option is to hand out cat treats to your friends to give your cat when he emerges from hiding. (Don't have them feed the cat from the dining table, though.) Give everyone a treat to hold in their hands. When your cat approaches a guest,

Shy cats need a place to get away.
(Photo courtesy of Cabitat)

he or she sets the treat down and allows kitty to eat it. The visitors should not try to touch the cat at all.

Ask your guests not to approach the cat, but to ignore him totally unless he approaches them. They may greet the cat by quietly using his name but should not presume to pet him unless he asks.

Watch your cat to be sure you aren't putting too much pressure on him. Don't insist that he tolerate every situation that occurs. If you have a big party or have boisterous friends over to visit, close the cat in a quiet room by himself.

Your cat may never be comfortable with some people, but he can learn that not all strangers are bad. Your friends will come to understand him better too, after you've enlisted their help.

Cats can be desensitized to certain loud noises in the same way. You can get tapes of thunderstorms, for instance, and play them softly as background noise while you feed your cat a treat. Increase the volume gradually and leave the tape on during meal times.

A trip to the veterinarian's office can be traumatic for a shy cat. Find out if any vets in your area perform house calls. If not, train your cat to travel in the car to eliminate stress in that part of the trip. See "Travel by Car." Ask your vet to schedule your visit for a slow time when there won't be many other people in the waiting room. Once you arrive, ask to be put into a quiet exam room immediately.

SLEEPING

Your cat needs more sleep than you do. Cats sleep for nine to twelve hours each day. A typical cat sleeps more at night than during the day.

Where does your cat sleep? On your bed, in his own bed, or just anywhere he can find? Cats like a soft, cozy place to sleep. They prefer a bed that is elevated above the floor and is located in a quiet place. An enclosed space sometimes makes the cat feel secure. Cats like small spaces such as sinks.

Many cats happily sleep with their owners. Some people can't sleep with cats, though. Perhaps you are allergic and the doctor has told you the cat has to stay out of the bedroom. Or your spouse can't sleep with a cat purring by his ear. Whatever the reason, you may be faced with telling your cat he can't sleep with you.

If you are getting a new kitten, training is easy. You just never let him sleep with you in the first place. Show the kitten his bed. Use a basket with a cushion inside, a hooded cat bed, or just a pillow in kitty's favorite spot. Close him in a room with the bed, food, and litter box so he has limited choices of where to sleep. The kitten quickly will find the softest spot and will develop a habit of sleeping there. Later you can decide whether to close him in that room every night or to close your bedroom door and let kitty have the run of the house.

Training an older cat not to sleep in the bedroom is a bit harder. The adjustment may be as hard on you as it is on your cat. Still, many people and their cats have made the change, and you can too. Brace yourself for a few weeks of transition, and realize that soon the new arrangement will feel normal to all.

Make sure your cat has a place of his own to sleep. If he can't be in bed with you, he needs his own bed. Rub some catnip on the bed so kitty likes it. Get some earplugs for yourself. Then close the bedroom door and go to sleep.

Cats like a warm, soft place to sleep.

Consider closing kitty in the room with his bed each night. This is just a temporary arrangement to condition him to sleep in his bed. It prevents kitty from keeping you awake by waving his paw plaintively under the bedroom door.

After a few sleepless nights listening to kitty meowing, you may wonder if the strain is worth it. Rest assured, though, that it does get better. See "Off-limits Furniture, Countertops, and Rooms" and "Meowing Too Much" for more tips. Before you know it, you will find your cat likes his new bed so much you catch him sleeping there in the daytime too.

STRAY CATS

Are you pestered by yowling tomcats in the neighborhood? Does a stray cat continually fight with yours? Do strays bother the birds in your bird feeder in the yard? You aren't totally helpless when it comes to managing stray cats. One of the following solutions may help.

Is your main problem with other outdoor cats that fight with yours? Since the main cause of fighting is sexual, you must get your cat spayed or neutered.

Neutering won't stop all fights, though. What's more, you can't get rid of every cat that may happen to fight with yours. The only solution is to keep your cat indoors. Everyone wants an easier fix for the problem, but there really isn't one. Keeping your cat indoors reduces veterinary bills significantly.

Even with your cat indoors, strays can still be a bother. Most "strays" are actually other people's pets that are let outdoors. If the stray cat is friendly, write a little note and tape it to its collar. Write something like "I saw your cat almost get hit by a

You can keep strays out of your yard.

car today. Please keep him indoors" or "Neutering your cat is cheaper than fixing the abscess he got by fighting with mine."

You also can set up harmless "booby traps" to scare cats out of your yard. Place an electronically controlled horn or siren in the yard. Attach an extension cord that leads indoors. Turn on the siren when the stray walks by.

Set up a water balloon to come splashing down on the cat when he walks by your window. Or lay duct tape, sticky side up, on the patio where he wanders. Turn on your sprinklers when you see the cat in your yard. Try to use a spigot where the cat can't see you turn it on.

Use your imagination and a little help from your local home electronics store. For instance, motion detectors work by turning on floodlights when motion is detected. You can have that system rewired so a 110 volt outlet goes where the floodlamps were. Then you can plug anything into that, and it will turn on when motion is detected. Consider plugging in your automatic sprinkler system or a portable tape player with a tape of dogs barking. Attaching a loud alarm also would scare a cat if the alarm is put right next to the place the cat walks. Be sure it is a self-limiting sound in case you aren't home when it goes off. All these are harmless ways to scare the stray out of your yard.

If the cats around your house are really homeless strays, do them a favor and take them to the nearest animal shelter. Stray cats live on the edge of starvation, so they are not better off left in the streets. They just reproduce and make more stray cats that continue to suffer.

Feeding strays may make you feel better, but that isn't a solution either. You will attract more strays, and they will continue to be neglected in other ways. Either take on the full responsibility of adopting them (vaccinating, neutering, and deworming), or do them a favor by taking them to the shelter.

Your local shelter may be able to lend you a trap that will catch the stray cat safely. The cat has a chance of being adopted from the shelter, a far better fate than continuing life as a stray.

TALKING TO YOUR CAT

After you spend time with any cat, you learn to tell what he is "saying" by his tone of voice, body language, and other subtle signals. Researchers have confirmed that cats have a language of their own. You can learn their language and become better at communicating with your cat.

The purr has several variations. Your cat may greet you with a short purr-meow sound. A request-purr is made for food or attention. A short murmur expresses expectation of a treat about to be received. And a long continuous purr shows contentment or satisfaction. Cats can purr so softly you can't hear the sound. They cannot purr when they are asleep.

What causes the purr sound? Researchers have argued for years about the origin of the purr. The current theory is that rapid contraction of the larynx and diaphragm muscles causes purring. This muscular activity creates air turbulence that produces the sound.

Open-mouthed sounds are variations of the meow, cry, and wail. "Meow" can be a demand, a cry for attention, a complaint, or an expression of bewilderment. Some cats give a silent meow when they want to be quiet but can't refrain from speaking.

The wail is used by kittens as a cry of distress when separated from their mother. The cry is a mating call. Tomcats give a caterwauling cry to announce their needs.

Sounds of anger or warning include the growl, snarl, hiss, and spit. Hissing warns a person or another cat not to come too close. Snarling accompanies active fighting.

Cats use body language along with sounds to show their feelings. When you greet your cat, he raises his tail in a friendly gesture. When a cat rolls over, he wants to play. (This is not usually a sign of submission as it is with dogs.)

Watch the cat's eyes for signs of his mood. Your cat's pupils dilate widely during play. He may leap sideways, stand on his hind feet, or crouch down and prepare to pounce. Biting and scratching are part of play behavior, but cats usually learn to retract their claws and control the strength of their bite. (See "Attacking People" or "Biting, Scratching, and Clawing People" for ways to teach your cat to play less roughly.)

Cats that are about to attack aggressively or defensively have a different attitude. They usually give plenty of warning before they attack. The cat's tail twitches and his hair stands on end, giving him a fluffed-up look. He may growl or hiss. If the cat is on the offensive, his ears will point forward. A frightened cat that takes the defense flattens his ears and arches his back.

Cats also use scent in communication. We can't smell the same things they do, but knowing about their use of scent helps us understand some of their behavior. This is especially true where their toilet habits are concerned. Cats mark their territory with urine.

Rubbing against objects or people is another way that cats leave their scent. No one can deny that cats enjoy being petted. But it is interesting to note that the areas cats like petted most also contain the most sebaceous glands. When you scratch your cat's chin or scratch his back just in front of his tail, you are taking up his scent.

Cats are extremely sensitive animals that are susceptible to stress. They prefer to have a consistent schedule and may become upset when that schedule changes. Cats also become attached to their home territory. Often they find it difficult to adjust to a new home.

A change in your cat's behavior is his way of telling you something is wrong. Psychological problems resulting from stress include urine spraying, loss of appetite, and excessive grooming. The solutions to each of these problems is discussed in their specific sections.

Do cats understand people language? Whether cats understand the words you say or your body language or a bit of both, it is clear to most people that their cats do understand what they say or feel. Cats can learn to obey commands too. A verbal command combined with a hand signal is especially effective.

Every cat needs a name. The more you use it, the more kitty will understand that it belongs to him alone. Say hello to your cat every time you see him. When you walk through the living room and kitty is sitting on the sofa, give him a little greeting. "Hi, Chester" is all you need, but it is enough that Chester knows you are talking to him. He might just open his eyes a bit or give a little murmur, but he does appreciate the attention.

Use your cat's name every time you pet him or feed him. He will learn to associate his name with wonderful experiences. Train your cat to come when you call. Whether he comes because he expects food or petting or because he just feels like coming, it is clear that he knows when you are calling.

Cats can learn many other words too. Although it takes a lot of work to teach a cat to sit, your cat quickly learns that when you tell your dog to sit and stay, the cat can tease the dog and get away with it without being chased.

Your cat can learn that "bedtime" means that you are going to bed, and he will run to his bed too. "Dinner" means food, and "outside" means you're taking a walk. Both the tone of your voice and the words convey meaning.

Cats are experts at reading body language. In fact, body language is more important to cats than verbal language. Your cat seems to "know" when you are going on vacation or leaving for work because he recognizes your actions. The cat may be responding to both your actions and your words, but either way, he understands your intent.

TEMPERATURE TAKING

Do you think your cat may be ill? Did you feel her nose and find it hot to the touch? Did your vet ask you to monitor kitty's temperature? In any case, a time will arise when you need to take your cat's temperature.

You may feel your cat's nose occasionally when you are concerned about her health. Unfortunately, the temperature of a cat's nose has nothing to do with her internal temperature. It is more likely related to whether kitty was sitting in the warm sun or in the shade. You will have to use a rectal thermometer to find out if kitty has a fever.

A human rectal thermometer or baby's thermometer will work for a cat. Shake down the mercury so it reads below 95 degrees. Lubricate the tip with petroleum jelly.

Have someone hold kitty's front end. Your handler may find it easiest to control the cat if she grasps the scruff of the neck with one hand. (Without lifting the cat—if you lift the feet off the ground, kitty will struggle.) Then you can lift kitty's tail and gently insert the thermometer about one inch. It helps to rotate the thermometer in rather than pushing it straight in. Hold the thermometer and the tail together in your hand so that when kitty moves, the thermometer and your hand move with her.

Leave the thermometer in for one or two minutes, then remove it and read the mercury level. The normal temperature for a cat is between 101 and 102 degrees Fahrenheit.

TOILET TRAINING

One way to get rid of the litter box is to train your cat to use the bathroom toilet. First, though, you have to decide whether you want your cat to learn this habit. The convenience could be offset by the problem of occasional misses and kitty footprints on the seat. Some cats may continue their scratching behavior and scratch the toilet seat. Once the cat is trained, you must always leave the bathroom door open, the toilet lid up, and the seat down.

Training your cat to use the toilet involves several separate steps. Wait to move from one step to the next until you are sure your cat understands what you want. There are several variations of the materials used here. Improvise and use what works best for you. Commercial training kits are available too. These contain some sort of pan that fits over the toilet bowl.

The whole idea is to make the toilet look like the litter box. Once kitty gets used to jumping up on the toilet to eliminate, then the material is removed and kitty just goes right into the toilet bowl. Wait to proceed with each step until your cat totally accepts each change.

First move kitty's litter box into the bathroom so he becomes accustomed to that room. Put it right next to the toilet. Wait several weeks until the litter box is being used habitually in that location.

Then put kitty's litter box on the toilet seat. Wait at least a week. Once kitty gets used to using it there, remove the box. Stretch some material or strong plastic over the toilet bowl and fasten it securely. Put litter in the center. Kitty should use this the same way he used the box. Gradually decrease the amount of litter you place there. Then poke some holes in the plastic so the urine can drain out. Finally, take away the material so kitty can just use the toilet.

An alternative plan also begins with placing the litter box

next to the toilet. Once the cat uses the box in that location, cover it with wire mesh that allows the stool and urine to drop through. Stretch the mesh over the box and bend the edges down so that it makes a sort of lid. Kitty will just eliminate right there on the wire since this is his box with the same location and smell as always. Again wait several weeks until using the wire over the box seems perfectly normal.

Then stretch some of the same wire over the toilet bowl. Put kitty up there and show him the wire. Then take away the regular box. When kitty goes into the bathroom looking for his litter box, pick him up and put him on the wire over the toilet bowl. Wait several weeks, again, until kitty is used to using the toilet. Your final step is to take the wire off the bowl.

A third method is to get an extra toilet seat and place it over the cat's litter box. Gradually reduce the amount of litter in the box. Then place the litter box–toilet seat combination on top of your toilet. Finally, remove the litter box and allow your cat to use the normal toilet seat.

No matter what method you use, if your cat has difficulty adjusting, go back to the previous step for another week. It may take time for kitty to understand what you want.

TRAINING BASICS

Of course cats are trainable. But can you train a cat like a dog? Absolutely not. Cats won't do something that doesn't make sense to them. Since they don't think like dogs, they can't be trained the same way.

People who are accustomed to training dogs may be stymied by a cat's behavior. Cats aren't any smarter or dumber than dogs, but they have different priorities and different ways of communicating.

You can't *make* a cat do anything, but you can try to make the cat *want to* do that thing. Training includes learning polite behavior (that is, not being bad) as well as learning tricks (following commands).

You will use positive reinforcement when teaching your cat to *do something,* such as sit or walk on a leash. Reserve punishment or negative reinforcement for times that you are teaching your cat *not to do something,* or for those times that kitty is getting in trouble. (Punishment can be a distraction and does not have to involve inflicting pain; see "Discipline and Disobedience.") There is no need to feel as if bad behavior is something you must "learn to live with." Unacceptable behavior *can* be changed.

Not only is bad behavior annoying, but it also may endanger the cat. For instance, many cats are poisoned when they inadvertently chew on toxic houseplants. Training your cat makes your life easier and the cat's life safer.

Very few of the cat's behavior "problems" are abnormal— that is, the behavior is normal to cats. Yet when it upsets you or disrupts your household, the behavior must change. When you understand why your cat misbehaves, you can train her to redirect her instincts in less destructive ways.

Cat behavior problems can be categorized loosely according to their cause. Knowing the cause helps you to understand and change the behavior.

Some behaviors we call "bad" are normal actions that are out of place. For instance, cats naturally want to sharpen their claws. You can't make that desire go away, but you can redirect the cat's attention from the furniture to a scratching post with a combination of discipline and rewards.

Another common cause of behavior problems is stress or frustration. Your cat may become stressed if you get another pet, change your working hours, buy a different brand of cat litter, or move her food bowl to a new spot. Cats that are overcrowded become stressed too. A stressed cat may stop using the litter box, meow constantly, or become destructive. Relieving the stress is essential to stop the behavior.

A third cause of behavior problems is inconsistent behavior on your part. Cats need to know that there are consistent rules in the house. For instance, you may allow kitty to jump on the table occasionally, but most of the time you yell at her when she does so. The result is confusion. Your cat doesn't know that you are torn between trying to be nice and trying to train her not to get on the table.

Another cause of bad behavior is improper socialization to other pets or to people. Kittens have specific ages when they learn to socialize with other cats and with humans. (See "Adopting Your Special Cat.") A cat that is not properly socialized may become stressed if she is later put into a situation where there are people of different ages coming and going, or where there are other pets in the household.

Inheritance also plays a role in various behavior tendencies. Although inheritance creates the basis for your cat's behavior, the environment you create is important in molding that behavior.

Certain behavior varies among breeds, with some cats being more vocal than others, some more playful, some more polite. Cats that are extremely inbred are more likely to have behavior problems. You can avoid this by carefully choosing the cattery from which you purchase a purebred cat.

Finally, there are medical reasons for abnormal behavior. Any sick cat will act depressed. Older cats with hyperthyroidism may be irritable.

Sometimes similar-appearing actions have very different causes with different solutions. It is important to examine closely when, how, and why your cat does what she does before you take any action. Specific hints are given in "Discipline and Disobedience" and under headings for each problem.

There is no reason to assume that you must live with objectionable behavior. If you aren't sure what is going on, or if your attempts at correcting the behavior meet with frustration, get some help. Start with a veterinarian to rule out any medical cause of the problem. Either a vet or an animal behavior specialist can help you with training and behavior problems.

Once your cat has been trained to be polite and understands the house rules, you can graduate to advanced training. This involves teaching your cat to obey commands or do tricks. Certain breeds of cats may learn tricks easier than others.

For instance, one study showed that Siamese, Abyssinian, and Himalayan cats apparently learn to fetch more often than cats of other breeds. Owners of Norwegian forest cats report that they naturally learn to fetch. But don't let a generalization keep you from training any kind of cat. Your cat will live up to your expectations—no less and no more.

Cats can be trained at any age, but you may find it easier to train a kitten. Wait until the kitten has gotten to know you and has shown he is able to pay attention.

Do you think your cat is too independent or too aloof to be trained? That is seldom the case. Aloof cats often act that way because their owners don't spend much time with them. So your first step is to increase the amount of time you spend with your cat—whether you are petting, talking to, or playing with him.

Realize that training takes time and effort. Decide how much you really want to train your cat before you start. It is impossible to train your cat without devoting a lot of attention to the task. You must be consistent and firm. Once you have committed yourself to training your cat, then you will begin to see results.

TRAINING: COME, SIT, OR FETCH

You need to give lots of positive reinforcement to train your cat to follow commands. What can you use? Scratch your cat's ears, rub his back, or pet him in his favorite spot. The most effective method is to use choice tidbits of food. Keep the amount small so you don't make kitty full.

Treats work best if they are special and different from the cat's ordinary food. Use a bit of canned food rolled into a small ball or a tiny piece of tuna. If your cat gets canned food free choice, then treats won't work as well as they would for a cat fed dry food. Do not give treats at any other time except when you are training. The treat must be given at the instant your cat takes the correct action.

When teaching commands, keep your training sessions at a short five to ten minutes to accommodate kitty's brief attention span. Start your training sessions in a quiet room with only you and the cat present—no other people or cats allowed. After kitty learns what to do, you can ask another person to join you. Repeat your training with the other person present.

All cats can learn to come when called. First, every cat needs a name that he recognizes. Use your cat's name every time you talk to him. Repeat his name when you are petting or playing with him.

Every time you refill the cat's food bowl, call his name. When you come home from work, give kitty a hello too. Try to use kitty's name with all sorts of positive experiences. Call your cat when he is already walking toward you. When he comes to you, give him an exuberant welcome and lots of petting.

When kitty is bad, use one of the distraction methods (see "Discipline and Disobedience") rather than calling his name. Never call your cat to punish him.

Every time you call your cat, give him loving, praise, and petting. If you want to hurry up the training or reinforce the

Every cat can learn to come when called.

come command, use a treat reward every time kitty comes to you. Keep a can of food in the refrigerator and take out a small ball of food.

Don't let kitty see you take the treat out of the refrigerator, or you will only train him to come when you open the fridge. Get the treat and leave the kitchen. Then call kitty's name, say "Come," and give him the treat and lots of praise when he arrives.

Soon your cat will realize that his name is associated with good things. He will come running every time he hears his name. Once you get a good response, continue to use treats only randomly to reinforce your training.

The sit up command is done with a food treat too. Hold the treat above kitty's head, make an upward sweeping motion with your other hand, and say, "Up." Since cats respond more to body language than words, it always helps to use a hand signal in addition to your command. If your cat swats at your hand, don't give the treat. Wait until he sits on his haunches to reward him.

Cats also can be taught to sit and stay. Start with sit, and don't progress to stay until the cat sits consistently. Push down on your cat's haunches to get him in a sitting position while you say "Sit." Give the treat only when kitty is in the sit position. You may need a helper to put the cat in a sit while you give the reward. Otherwise the cat will stand up as soon as you reach for the treat.

Use a table in a corner of the room to reduce the chances of your cat's breaking the sit. A collar and lead provide a bit of control too.

Work with the sit command daily until you get a good response. Then put your cat in a sit and hold your hand out in front of his face in a halt gesture and say, "Stay." Keep your hand right in front of his face so he can't get up. At first, give the reward after just a few seconds. Gradually increase the time that elapses between your stay command and the reward. Use some sort of release command to tell your cat when the stay is over.

Many cats know how to fetch. Some seem to learn naturally, some must be trained, and some never understand. A cat must first show a tendency to pick up toys in his mouth. Begin by playing with your cat using something he can pick up in his mouth—a small sponge ball or wad of paper. Tease and tempt kitty with the paper first. Throw the paper a short distance, say "Fetch," and allow kitty to pick it up. As soon as he drops it, pick it up rather than letting him play with it. Squeeze it in your hand to get his attention and throw it again.

Attach a string to the toy to make it easier to retrieve. Gradually pull the cat in if he picks up the toy but doesn't come to you. If kitty doesn't pick it up, pull on the string and tease him back toward you. Once the cat and toy arrive at your feet, pick up and throw the toy again. Each time you pick up the toy, give kitty lots of praise.

Your cat may decide to do one of his tricks even when you don't ask. That may be cute, but don't give him a treat unless you first asked him to perform. Otherwise the tables will turn and he will be training you.

TRAINING: IS KITTY TRAINING *YOU*?

Cats are much better at training their owners than you may think. Sometimes the result is innocuous enough: Your cat meows, so you pick her up. Other situations can be a bother.

For instance, a woman says about her overweight cat, Bart: "I can't get my cat to eat dry food. He just meows all the time, so I have to give him the canned food." Bart has trained her to feed canned food when he meows. Other cats use pitiful looks for the same result.

Another man says he is getting frustrated with his cat's demands to be let in and out. "I no sooner sit down than Tiger meows to be let out. Then a few minutes later he's meowing at the window, wanting back in again."

Tiger gets great amusement watching his owner get up to let him in and out. He has trained his owner to open the door when he meows. A cat door would solve that problem.

Naughtier yet, another cat wakes her owners at 5:30 A.M. each day. They endure the plaintive meows for as long as they can, then finally get up and feed her. She has trained them quite well! If they fed her at night, instead, her habit would soon stop. They should get up and close the cat in the bathroom as soon as she meows.

There is nothing wrong with your cat training you, as long as you recognize what she's doing and are an agreeable trainee. But don't let your cat manipulate you to get what she wants. If your cat is that good at training you, she must be smart enough that you can train her too.

TRANQUILIZING FOR TRAVEL

Imagine you are moving across the country and taking your cats with you in the car. They both meow constantly when you drive. Is there anything you can do to make the trip easier?

You can endure meowing for a short trip to the vet's, but on a longer drive the noise could drive you nuts. What's more, you constantly worry over kitty's misery.

Start by training your cats to ride in the car. The more they are used to driving, the easier the trip will be. (See "Travel by Car.")

Some cats still meow constantly, though. Your veterinarian can prescribe a mild tranquilizer or antinausea medication to help your cat tolerate a long drive. Every cat reacts differently to tranquilizers. You want your cat to be relaxed but not totally asleep. Consider giving half the dose, then waiting to see how your cat responds before giving the rest.

You also could ask your vet for an extra "trial" dose that you can give the week before you leave to see how your cat reacts. Then you can reduce the dose on travel day if your cat is especially responsive to the drug. Be cautious in extreme temperatures. Tranquilized cats are less able to regulate their body heat in either hot or cold temperatures.

Most cats need only one dose of a tranquilizer for a full day of travel. Although the drug wears off before the end of the day, the cat has become accustomed to the drive and remains calm.

If your cat will be traveling by air, call the airline ahead of time to find out their specific requirements. Some airlines do not want animals to be tranquilized while they are airborne.

TRAVEL BY CAR

Are you planning to take your cat somewhere in the car? Do you dread visits to the veterinarian because your cat raises such a fuss? Whether kitty is going for a ride across town or across the state, you want to make the trip as uneventful as possible. Some cats travel well, while others become stressed at the shortest ride. You can train your cat to tolerate riding in the car.

First consider the way your cat feels about the car. Do you

Cardboard carriers are inexpensive and handy.

use it only to take her to the vet's? Small wonder kitty doesn't like the car. You need to take the cat for drives that she enjoys too.

Your cat will feel much more secure if she is in a carrier in the car. There are carriers to fit every need and budget. Small cardboard carriers with a handle are economical and excellent for short trips to the vet's office. These can be reused and are more escape-proof than a simple cardboard box. For longer trips, get a carrier with "windows" so kitty can look out.

Expose kitty to the carrier in your home well before you plan to use it in the car. Leave it open so she can jump in. Make the carrier into a bed, or put your cat's food or some catnip inside. Then when you put kitty in it for travel, the carrier won't be part of what she fears. In fact, it might make her feel much better than being loose in the car.

To start your car training, take kitty (in her carrier) to the car and sit with her there without driving. Give her a treat. Then try taking her for short rides to nowhere and returning home.

Start by just going around the block. Put some catnip in the carrier before you start. Give kitty lots of praise during the whole drive. Stop halfway around the block and give kitty a treat. Give another when you return, while you are still in the car. Repeat the process daily, then weekly as your cat becomes accustomed to the car.

All cats must have a collar and identification tag. By the time kitty gets away it doesn't do any good to say "But she never got away before, so I didn't think I needed a collar!" You can't predict what loud noise, big dog, or other distraction will cause your cat to panic and run away. There are plenty of safety collars made for cats, if you are concerned that your cat will get caught on something.

If you are traveling to another state, you need to get a health certificate from your veterinarian within a week of your departure. This form states that the cat was examined and found to be free from disease. Also take a copy of your cat's rabies certificate and evidence of other vaccinations. Although you won't often be asked to present these documents, the law requires that you carry them.

Car travel problems include meowing and motion sickness. Meowing is usually a sign of stress. Reduce stress by training your cat to ride in a carrier in the car. For long trips, consider using a tranquilizer or catnip to reduce your cat's anxiety.

Kittens that get car sick usually grow out of the problem. To reduce car sickness, withhold food or feed less than normal on the morning of the car ride. Drive slowly and take turns carefully. Adult cats that continue to get car sick can be given medication prescribed by your vet.

Long trips pose a challenge for some people and their cats. Many cats will not eat or drink while traveling. Water intake is more important than food intake. Offer canned food, since this contains lots of water. Avoid traveling in the heat of the day. (See "Hot Weather and Overheating.")

Even if you are able to drive all day and night, it is best to plan stay-overs in motels for the cat's sake. Several major motel chains allow pets. (See appendix, under "Books.") The stop-over allows your cat to eat and drink if she didn't do so in the car. If your cat is tranquilized for the drive, give only one dose in the morning. It should wear off by evening, when you are in your motel room. Then your cat will be interested in eating and drinking. Set up her litter box too. Put a DO NOT DISTURB sign on your door if you leave the room so the maid doesn't accidentally let kitty loose. Or confine kitty in her carrier when you leave the room.

TRAVEL BY PLANE

Cats can travel on airplanes as baggage or as passengers. Most people prefer taking their cat as a passenger. You have to travel with the cat in this case. Be sure to make your reservations well ahead of time, since only a few animals are allowed in the passenger cabin on each flight.

Ask the airline about the specific requirements for a carrier. The type and exact size of carrier are strictly controlled. If you show up with the wrong kind you may be turned away or forced to buy one from the airline (if they have any).

The carrier must fit under the seat. The cat must be able to stand up and turn around in the carrier. You are not allowed to take the cat out of the carrier during the entire flight, but you can put the carrier on your lap and talk to your cat.

Reduce stress by getting your cat accustomed to the carrier well before the trip. Put a treat or some catnip in the carrier at home to encourage kitty to go inside. Then leave it open so your cat can explore.

Cats also can go as "excess baggage." Here, again, you should make an early reservation and ask about specific requirements for the type of carrier. Find out how pets are handled. Some airlines load pets on last and unload them first so they don't have to sit in the cargo area for long. Try to book a direct, nonstop flight to avoid the chance of your cat missing a plane or enduring delays. Be sure someone is available to pick up the cat immediately upon arrival.

Ask the airline about their "heat policy." In the summer, airlines won't take pets on board if the temperature at the departure or destination is over about 80 degrees. This is for your cat's safety, but it can be a problem since the temperature won't be known until the time of takeoff.

To avoid temperature problems, reserve a flight early in the morning or late in the evening. Avoid routes that go through

Each airline has specific requirements for cat carriers.
(Photo courtesy of Sherpa Bags)

the southern states if you have a choice. Book a direct flight, if possible, so the cat doesn't have to wait in a hot, stuffy cargo area while switching planes.

Cold temperatures also can be a problem. Your cat may be turned away at the airport if the temperature is too low. If your cat may get cold, put a fluffy blanket in the carrier. Choose a daytime route through warm southern states.

Get a collar and identification tag for your cat. Use the collar well before you leave so your cat is accustomed to it. Feed your cat lightly the morning of travel. A full stomach could make the trip less comfortable. Be sure to take the cat's health certificate, rabies vaccination certificate, and evidence of other vaccinations with you to the airport. Your cat will not be allowed on the flight without them.

The health certificate is not the same as the rabies certificate. The health certificate is a document filled out by a veterinarian to show the cat is free of any infectious disease. The cat must be examined and the certificate filled out within a week of departure.

Flights to other countries require long-range planning. You must inquire about the destination country's requirements for pets. Sometimes the required paperwork takes several weeks to complete. Some countries require that certain animals be quarantined when they arrive. Your veterinarian, the country's consulate, or your state veterinarian's office has more information.

URINATING IN THE BATHTUB

Some cats like to use the tub or shower for their litter box. Perhaps the shiny surface appeals to them. Whatever the reason for your cat's preference, the habit is an easy one to stop.

Simply fill the tub with an inch or two of water. Do this for several weeks until kitty assumes that the tub always will have water in it. You may have to repeat the lesson occasionally if kitty tries again several months later.

It may be that your cat prefers a smooth surface to his litter. Try using no litter, less litter, or a sand litter in the box. Once the cat uses the box with no litter in it, you can put litter back in gradually.

Filling the tub with water may just make your cat use the floor near the tub for his toilet. If that happens, place his litter box next to the tub so he can use the litter in a place he likes. Wait until kitty uses the box without a problem. Then gradually move the box back toward the location you want it to stay.

This method also works in cases where the cat prefers another specific place in the house for his toilet. Simply make that spot inaccessible (by placing the cat food there or putting a cactus there) and place the litter box close by. Or place the litter box over that spot. Usually the cat will begin to use the box immediately. You can leave the box there or, if you want it elsewhere, slowly move it a little bit each day until it is back where it started.

URINATING OUTSIDE THE BOX

Is your cat urinating outside of the box? The behavior has many causes, so you must look further to figure out what is going on. Sometimes the cat has watery diarrhea and urinating isn't the main problem; when the cat strains to defecate, he urinates too. If the primary problem is urine, you must differentiate between a break in toilet habits and spraying.

Spraying is a sexual or territorial marking behavior. The cat squirts urine in a forceful stream on walls or other vertical surfaces while standing. Cats back up to a wall and twitch their tails while spraying. Both male and female cats spray, but males do so more often. See "Urine Spraying" for tips on that problem.

Urinating is done in the squatting position onto a horizontal surface. Usually a normal amount of urine is voided, and the cat makes scratching motions afterward. Cats that urinate outside the box have developed poor toilet habits or have a medical problem.

Although the two behaviors seem obviously different at first, some cats urinate (rather than spray) to mark their territory. *Urine marking* is done for the same reasons as spraying. Marking is done in a squatting position, but the cat does not void a normal amount of urine. Instead, he voids only a small amount, to "mark" the area with his scent. Usually the cat does not scratch to cover the urine. See "Urine Spraying" for tips on reducing the incidence of urine marking.

Now that you have the basic types of urine problems defined, let's focus on *urination:* poor toilet habits or medical problems. There are several potential causes of urinating outside the box. The first step in solving your cat's urination problem is to have him examined by your vet.

Urinary tract infection or inflammation (feline urological syndrome [FUS] or cystitis) is extremely common in cats. Signs include frequent urination, urinating outside the box, or straining to urinate. A cat can become blocked so that urine doesn't pass. This is an emergency that requires an immediate call to your veterinarian, no matter what time of day or night.

FUS usually is controllable with a change in diet. New research has revealed better ways to manage FUS, leaving much of the old advice obsolete. Be sure to consult with your vet about the best way to manage your cat's problem and the proper food to use.

Some cats have recurring urinary tract disorders. Even if a cat was treated for the problem a few weeks ago, it could recur at any time. Some people neglect to treat repeated urinary tract infections because they inadvertently assume the cat has a behavior problem. Even if your cat was seen by a vet and treated, return to the vet if the problem had cleared but now has returned.

Only after a medical cause is ruled out should you worry about your cat's behavior. Cats may urinate outside the box when they don't like the box or the litter for some reason. They may or may not defecate outside the box too.

Cats demand cleanliness in their toilet. Do you clean the box often enough? Remove the feces daily and change the litter at least once a week or as soon as an odor is apparent.

Is the box in a quiet location? Do you have dogs that bother your cat while he's using the box? Place the box in a low-traffic area. The laundry room is a common location for the litter box but may be too noisy if you do a lot of laundry. Consider using more than one box if you have more than two cats or a large house.

You may find that your cat prefers the box to be up high rather than on the floor. This will make cleaning easier for you too. It also keeps the dog out of the litter box.

Is the box big enough for your cat? A large cat needs a large box. Is the box covered? Although covered boxes have several advantages, some cats refuse to use them. Is the box too close to the cat's food? Some cats won't eliminate near their dinner.

Cats are choosy about their litter. Behaviors that indicate

your cat may not like the litter include shaking the paws, strad-
dling the box to avoid touching the litter, or digging outside of
the box on the floor or wall. A cat that uses one specific area in
the house instead of his box is likely to have an aversion to the
litter or the box you are using.

Studies show that cats prefer sand-type litter or clay litter
with a fine consistency. Dusty or perfumed litter, or litter with
large particles, is not liked as well. Many cats use unperfumed,
dust-free clay litter without trouble. Once you find a brand of
litter that your cat likes, don't switch brands. If you must switch,
gradually blend the new with the old to help kitty adjust.

It may be necessary to change to an entirely different type of
litter if your cat doesn't like the litter you now use. For instance,
if you use a clay litter, then your cat's problem may not improve
with a change to a different brand of clay litter. Instead, try
switching to a sand litter, sawdust, wood chips, or alfalfa pellets.
Consider setting out several litter boxes with different types of
litter in them to allow your cat to choose the one he likes best.

Whether the problem was a dirty litter box or a disliked litter,
simply making changes may not be enough to entice your cat
back to the box. He has developed a habit of using other surfaces, and now you must retrain him to use the box. Thoroughly
remove the odor in the places he has used, then read "Litter
Box Training and Type of Litter."

Some cats choose one particular area of your home in which
to urinate. You need to make that spot less desirable than the
litter box. Since cats prefer to dig in a rough surface, cover the
area with foil or plastic wrap. Cover a large area so the cat
doesn't just use the spot next to your foil.

Most cats don't like citrus scent, so you could put a lemon-
scented air freshener in the spot. Or put the cat food dish there
temporarily. Cats usually don't urinate where they eat.

At the same time, make the litter box more desirable to the
cat by changing the litter type, keeping the box cleaner, and so
on. Remember that the cat may not realize you've improved the
box until you show him. You may need to put the litter box in

the area your cat has been using until your cat uses the box routinely. Leave it there for several weeks. (You can remove it temporarily when you have company and need to use the room.) Then, inch by inch, slowly move it back to its old location. Be patient. If you move too fast your cat will go back to his old habits.

Does your cat urinate on your bed? The cat may prefer the texture of the bed, or he may be urine-marking. (See "Urine Spraying.") A cat that urinates on the bed only when you are away may suffer from separation anxiety. (See "Depression, Boredom, and Loneliness.")

Any emotional upset can cause a cat to stop using his box. Your move to a new home, recent marriage, or change in your working hours may disturb your cat. Establish a regular and consistent schedule as soon as possible to reduce the stress in kitty's life.

Your veterinarian may prescribe antianxiety medication for a short time to help your cat adjust to a sudden change or stress in his life. Using medicine doesn't mean you can ignore all the other advice presented here. Drugs are just another aid in your training. Once kitty settles down, the medication can be withdrawn and the problem usually doesn't recur.

What should you do when you catch your cat in the act of urinating outside the box? Use punishment cautiously because often it can backfire. Be sure your cat doesn't have a medical urinary disorder before you begin to think about modifying his behavior.

Once you are certain your cat is healthy, you can use aversion techniques to help retrain him to the box. Make a loud noise or squirt him with water *when you catch him in the act* of soiling outside the litter box. Then put him in the room with the litter box and close the door. Be careful that your cat does not begin to associate the box with punishment. Don't ever force him into the box or hold him there.

Remember that you cannot tell your cat what he did wrong after the fact. Use aversion techniques only when you catch your cat in the act of urinating outside the box. And be sure you are considering the factors mentioned above (location, litter type) to make the box more appealing to your cat.

URINE SPRAYING

Spraying or marking is the cat's way of establishing his territory. Spraying is often done near doors and windows, on beds, or on new items. Most cats mark vertical surfaces when spraying urine. Sometimes the cat will mark in a squatting position. Read "Urinating Outside the Box" if you aren't certain whether your cat is spraying or urinating.

The most effective way to stop a male cat from spraying is to have him neutered. This is 80 to 90 percent effective, even in older cats. No matter what your cat's age, neutering is the first step to take with a spraying problem.

Intact females also may spray. They should be spayed since the problem worsens when they are in heat. But why do altered male or female cats still spray urine?

Urine spraying has nothing to do with the litter box itself. Cats that spray won't be helped by changing the box or the litter.

Spraying or marking with urine may begin or worsen when a new cat is added to the house. You can prevent some problems by slowly introducing the new cat. (See "Introducing Cats.")

Let the cats have plenty of personal space by providing cat trees and houses with lots of places to hide. Perches, walkways, and kitty condos also help decrease the feeling of crowding.

Provide more than one food bowl and litter box so the cats are not forced together.

Spraying is much more likely to occur in homes with several cats. It can occur even if you already had more than one cat and previous additions were tolerated well. There is a point where cats begin to feel overcrowded, and that is when they will begin to spray. Sometimes the only solution is to reduce the number of cats in the home. The cat that is spraying the most may stop if he is put in a home where he is the only cat.

Your cat may spray near a door or window where he can see an outdoor cat pass by. This can be a hidden cause of a cat's sudden onset of spraying. If this seems to be the problem, try to block your cat's view of the other cat. (See "Stray Cats" for more tips.)

Some cats spray in just one area of the home. Try putting your cat's food and water dishes there to deter the spraying. This works only if your cat has chosen one particular spot he prefers to spray. Otherwise he will just spray elsewhere.

Sometimes a cat will urinate on one person's clothing or bed. If your cat seems to dislike and single out one person in the house as a target, try having that person be the only one to feed the cat. That may help the cat accept the person better. When this problem occurs only when you are not home, the cat may have separation anxiety. (See "Depression, Boredom, and Loneliness.") With separation anxiety, the cat may soil the clothing of the person he misses most.

A cat may begin to spray if he feels stressed for any other reason too. No matter what the cause, don't let the spraying continue without taking action. The longer the cat continues the behavior, the harder it will be to stop.

Putting a "diaper" on the cat may be a temporary solution to the house soiling caused by spraying. Make one yourself or use a commercially made cat diaper.

Sometimes medication is used to halt the spraying. This halts the cat's behavior while you relieve the stress or the cat becomes accustomed to whatever change has occurred. Then the dose of medicine is reduced gradually until the cat behaves normally without treatment or on a very low dose of medication.

Don't wait until the problem has existed for months before "finally resorting" to medication. It is important to break the spraying cycle as quickly as possible so it doesn't become a habit. At the same time, you can't rely on medication alone to solve your problem. It is essential that you find the reason for the cat's spraying. Your veterinarian can help you do this.

Be sure to thoroughly clean any place the cat has sprayed. Wash the entire wall and soak the carpet with a product that neutralizes urine odor.

VACATIONING WITH KITTY

Imagine your family is taking a two-week vacation this summer in your new RV. You can't decide what to do with your cat, since you can't stand the thought of leaving Bert alone for all that time. What should you do?

Consider whether Bert's personality is suited to travel. Some cats travel well while others are less tolerant of riding in vehicles. Shy or fearful cats won't enjoy a vacation. Elderly or sick cats should stay home too. An outgoing, healthy, and calm cat might enjoy a vacation as much as you do.

Take some trial runs to see whether your cat will travel well. First spend some time in the parked car or RV with kitty. Then take him for short drives to see how he behaves. (See "Travel by Car.")

Your travel plans also affect your decision to bring your cat. If you will be traveling in the hot southern states, your cat might suffer from the heat—especially if you park the RV and leave him there for long periods. On the other hand, kitty might enjoy himself on a leisurely trip in cooler areas. Call ahead to be sure cats are allowed at the places you plan to stay. (See appendix.)

Consider leash-training your cat before you leave. Your vacation will be much more pleasant if you can take him for walks rather than leaving him cooped up in the RV all the time. Get a harness collar rather than just the kind that goes around the cat's neck. Your cat will be more comfortable and less likely to slip out and escape.

Even if you don't leash-train your cat, it is essential that he wear an identification collar at all times. No matter how sure you are that he won't escape, that one exception will haunt you forever. Put a friend's phone number on the tag in addition to your own since you won't be home to receive any calls.

Have your cat's vaccinations updated before you leave. If you will be traveling across state lines, you also will need a health certificate. This document, which is not the same as a rabies certificate, certifies that your veterinarian has examined your cat and found him free of contagious disease. The exam must be performed shortly before your departure.

Take along several of your cat's toys as well as his usual food, dishes, grooming tools, and litter pan. Take your cat's bed too. And always take a cat carrier.

A cat let loose in your vehicle can get under your feet when you are driving or can slip out the door when you make a rest stop. Get a large cat carrier so your cat is comfortable. Then let kitty get used to it well before you leave. (See "Travel by Car.")

Perhaps you have decided not to take your cat along after all. Can you leave your cat home alone? Many cats fare well for a day or two when left with plenty of food and water. They need to be boarded or to have a cat-sitter for longer vacations. (See "Boarding" and "Cat-sitter.")

VETERINARIAN SELECTION AND REDUCING KITTY'S STRESS

Your cat needs a regular doctor who knows her personality quirks and special health problems. Veterinary care ranges from low-cost, corner-cutting basic service to fancy hospitals with specialists on staff. Chances are that something in between those two extremes will be just right for you and your cat.

Look for a veterinarian before you need one. You can't choose a veterinarian quickly, with just a perusal of the yellow pages and a few phone calls to check prices. Your cat's health deserves more than that. Start your search by asking friends and neighbors who they use and why they like their vet. Consider your priorities too. Is a nearby location essential? Do you always want to see the same vet, or is it okay if one of several associates sees your cat at different visits?

Is emergency service available? Veterinarians in many communities pool their resources and trade emergency on-call days. While you won't always get your own vet during off-hours, this ensures that someone is always available. A vet who takes his or her own emergency calls may not answer the phone every time, since it is impossible to be everywhere at once.

Once you have the names of several veterinarians, call each of them and ask for a hospital tour. Note how long it takes them to answer the phone and appraise the receptionist's attitude.

Expect no less from your veterinarian and veterinary hospital than you do from your own physician. The hospital should be clean and odor-free. A separate, spotless room should be available for surgery, and the surgeon should wear a cap, mask, and sterile gown when operating.

Look at the hospital cages and the animals. Are they clean? Is an isolation ward available for contagious patients? Is there a separate area for cats, away from the dogs? Perhaps there is a cats-only clinic in your area. Cats are much more relaxed at the vet's when they can't see, hear, or smell dogs.

Are appointments required? If you want the convenience of drop-in service, be ready for the trade-off: possible long delays in a waiting room full of people and other pets.

Does the hospital provide educational handouts explaining various diseases and behavior problems? Does it send out yearly reminders for vaccinations? What health program does it suggest for your cat? Be sure that everything is explained adequately. Are the staff friendly, helpful, and knowledgeable?

You are probably concerned about prices too. But you get what you pay for in veterinary care. The rock-bottom lowest prices are possible only by cutting corners: reusing surgical packs without sterilization between animals, not taking the time to examine animals before they're vaccinated, using untrained personnel instead of qualified veterinary technicians, or omitting a laboratory for performing basic tests. (Although most hospitals will send blood to an outside lab for extensive testing, the hospital should be able to perform complete blood counts, urinalysis, and fecal exams on the premises.)

Of course, there are price-gougers in veterinary medicine just as there are in other fields. Choose a vet who comes highly recommended and avoid the cheapest in town, and you will probably be satisfied.

Even if you are happy with your vet, your cat may not be. Does your cat hide on the morning of her veterinarian's appointment? (The cat senses your stress or sees the carrier.) Does she meow through the entire drive to the clinic? Do you get scratched trying to get kitty to hold still on the table? Some people stop taking their cats to the vet because the trip is so traumatic. But that doesn't solve anything, since health problems will inevitably arise.

Most cats can learn to at least tolerate a visit to the vet's. First, examine your own reactions. Is your cat picking up your own nervousness or worry? Your attitude must be that this is a relaxed routine, nothing more. If you are afraid of needles, don't assume that your cat is too, or she may fulfill your prophesy.

Now consider the car ride. Is this where kitty reacts the most? That isn't unexpected, if the only time she rides in the car is when she is going to the vet's. Try taking her for short rides at other times, just to teach her that riding in the car isn't a terrible thing. (See "Travel by Car.")

Your cat absolutely *must* have a cat carrier when riding in the car. The carrier helps her feel more secure. Even if your cat rides quietly, you still need the carrier to hold the cat in the parking lot and waiting room.

If your cat hates the carrier (because she knows that the only time you use it is when she goes to the vet's), then leave it open and feed her in it at home. Some people use their cat's carrier as her bed, so the cat loves riding in the carrier.

The next consideration is your veterinarian's office and the people there. Is the waiting room stressful for your cat because it is filled with barking dogs? Perhaps the staff will put your cat's carrier in a place where there is less commotion while you wait to be seen. Ask to schedule your appointment during a slow time of day.

Are the veterinarians and the staff calm and soft-spoken? An especially timid cat needs quiet, calm handling. Is there a cats-only clinic in your area? Cats are much more relaxed in these clinics.

If you have an aversion to needles, leave the exam room while your cat gets her shots. Cats usually endure the needle prick much easier than their owners, but they can feel your anxiety and will become more stressed.

Finally, consider using a house-call veterinarian. House calls are available in many areas, and this solution could be the best for both you and your cat.

VITAMINS AND OTHER SUPPLEMENTS

Is your cat a bit lethargic or underweight? Do you think she might perk up a little if you gave her a vitamin? Before you reach for a box of kitty vitamins, consider your goal and whether a vitamin will be the answer.

Cats don't suffer from the same dietary problems people do from eating fast foods and skipping meals. Good quality commercial cat foods contain more than enough vitamins and minerals, so healthy cats don't need extra.

When a cat is lethargic, she may just need the stimulation of extra play time. If her coat is scruffy, she may need a better-quality food. If she is too thin or isn't feeling well, she needs a veterinary examination.

Some people on a budget purchase an inexpensive, generic brand of cat food. Then, wondering whether their cat is getting enough nutrition, they buy a vitamin supplement.

Trying to supplement a poor diet is a guessing game where your cat comes out the loser. A better and less costly alternative is to just purchase a good-quality food in the first place. Then you know your cat is getting all the essential nutrients.

Another person might feed his cat a good-quality food plus a supplement, in a misdirected effort to give the cat every possible health advantage. Yet supplementing a balanced diet may only upset the balance of nutrients in the food. Feeding a good-quality food plus a balanced vitamin supplement will give your cat 200 percent of his daily requirement of vitamins. That's probably not enough to cause toxicity, but it is a waste of your money.

Still another cat owner may notice that her cat has a scruffy coat or has lost weight. She begins to give him a supplement, thinking perhaps that will help. Yet she is likely to find that a month later, the cat is still doing poorly.

If you think your cat doesn't look healthy, ask your vet to

look her over to find out what could be wrong. Adding a vitamin supplement may only prolong the time until your cat's real problem is diagnosed and treated.

Pregnant and nursing cats need more energy and higher levels of some nutrients. Pregnant cats eat about one-quarter more, and nursing cats eat two times more, than a normal adult cat. Feed dry kitten food ("growth" food) free choice to pregnant or nursing cats to give them the nutrition they need. That will provide a better balance of nutrients than will adding a supplement.

Cats that are too thin but aren't sick need to eat more. You can "supplement" your cat's diet with more cat food. Feed canned food (if the flavor encourages your cat to eat more) or kitten food to help your cat gain weight. (See "Weight Loss" for more tips.)

Aren't there some supplements that are relatively harmless, though? What about wheat germ oil or brewer's yeast? Wheat germ oil is a good source of vitamin E, but cat food should contain plenty if it is good quality and hasn't been stored too long. Brewer's yeast contains B vitamins, which also should be plentiful in cat food. Your cat will pass extra B vitamins in her urine when she has enough. Neither of these supplements is harmful to your cat, although the wheat germ oil could make her gain weight.

Cats that have suffered from urinary problems sometimes receive a urinary acidifier as a supplement. These are used less often now than in the past because diets made for the problem already promote an acid urine. It is possible to make a diet too acidic. If you feed a special diet to your cat, you could make her sick by adding a urinary acidifier. Your vet can check your cat's urine acidity to see if a supplement is necessary.

Cats that are stressed or ill need more nutrients. The supplement they need depends on their illness or type of stress. If there is a severe need, then the cat is likely hospitalized and is receiving intravenous fluids that contain a variety of vitamins and electrolytes.

Usually, though, when extra nutrients are needed, veterinarians prefer that cats take in those nutrients in their ordinary food. With all the special therapeutic diets now available, most veterinarians will chose a diet change before they prescribe a vitamin supplement. Special diets contain all the extra vitamins needed for a particular illness, plus they contain nutrients in exactly the correct proportions for your cat.

With all that said, there are still times when vitamins are required. Your veterinarian will advise you about what special food should be offered and whether a supplement is necessary.

VOMITING, BULIMIA, HAIRBALLS

Every cat owner has seen a cat vomit once or twice. If your cat throws up once but appears otherwise healthy, wait and see what happens. A cat that isn't eating, that acts sick, or that otherwise worries you should go to the vet. And any cat that vomits more than once in a day or that does so more than once a week needs medical attention.

Sometimes cats will vomit when they are not sick. Gulping food, eating odd things, and hairballs are common causes of vomiting related to the cat's behavior. There are many other different causes of vomiting, though, so don't make assumptions regarding the cause of your cat's reaction. How can you tell when there is a problem?

Some cats don't have a health problem, just a minor upset tummy. Outdoor cats eat anything from grasshoppers to mice, and occasionally some tidbit upsets their stomachs.

Greedy or hungry cats may gulp their food and regurgitate it, undigested, shortly thereafter. (It's not really bulimia, but it

Regular grooming of long-haired cats prevents hairballs.
(Photo courtesy of Advent Hill Cattery)

seems that way.) If your cat gulps his food, you can try feeding smaller and more frequent meals. Or put food in several different places to slow his eating. Try putting several round, smooth stones, each about one to two inches in diameter, in with his dry food. (Make sure they are big enough that they won't fit in his mouth and be accidentally swallowed, but small enough to move around in the bowl.) Your cat will have to pick around the stones to eat.

Another common cause of vomiting is hairballs. You can tell this is the problem by looking at what comes up. Sometimes the cat won't vomit but instead will develop a raspy cough. The cat looks as if he is trying to get something out of his throat, and he is—hair. Cats with a "hairball cough" will stretch out their necks and make a honking cough that ends with gagging.

If your cat has vomited hair, use a hairball remedy to help move the hair through the cat's intestines. There are many brands, and some cats prefer certain flavors over others. They all are laxatives with similar ingredients—petroleum jelly flavored with something good. (See "Shedding Excessively.")

Follow your vet's or the label's instructions on using the hairball remedy. Usually the product is used daily for several days and then repeated once weekly. Don't use it daily for more than a few days, however, since it could interfere with digestion or absorption of nutrients. If you use a hairball remedy for a couple of days and your cat continues to vomit or cough, take him to the vet for a checkup.

Hairballs are more common in long-haired cats and are especially frequent during shedding seasons—the spring and fall. To prevent hairballs, brush your cat frequently to get the hair off before kitty grooms it all off himself—right into his stomach.

Gulping food and hairballs are two common causes of vomiting where you can help your cat yourself. But if you aren't sure what the problem is, ask your vet to examine the cat to verify your suspicions. If your cat is sick for more than a day, don't fiddle around with home remedies—take him to the vet.

Although cats are desert animals, they still need fresh water.
(Photo courtesy of Cabitat)

WATER

Cats are funny about water. They are picky about where they drink and may decide to drink anywhere except their dish. Some cats have an annoying habit of tipping over water glasses. Cats may like to play with water, but they don't enjoy being bathed.

Water is an often-overlooked essential nutrient. Cats need water every day, but sometimes they are choosy about their water source. They want only the freshest, cleanest water, and they like having several choices of where to drink.

Although modern cats' ancestors were adapted to living in the North African desert, they still need plenty of fresh water to drink. The average cat needs to drink just under a cup of water per day. Canned cat food provides a lot of water, so cats fed canned food may not drink very much.

Keep your cat's water bowl scrupulously clean. The water will stay freshest in a stainless steel, heavy glass, or porcelain bowl rather than a plastic one. Provide more than one water bowl if your house is large. Cats that go outdoors need an outside water dish too. Change the water daily even if the bowl is still full. Placing water dishes near the sink will help you stay conscientious about this chore.

Many cats prefer to drink out of the faucet. Cats may prefer cold water. Some cat owners keep a jug of water in the refrigerator and fill the bowl from that. Others place an ice cube in the cat's water bowl. Some say that their cats prefer the taste of purified water. Experiment to find out how your cat prefers his water.

Some cats play with their water. Using a large, untippable water dish helps prevent a mess all over the floor. If your cat likes to tip over cups of water, you cannot leave them out. Try setting a "booby trap" to help train the cat not to bother your water. (See "Discipline Tools.")

WEIGHT LOSS

Is your cat too thin or losing weight? Sometimes the problem is obvious, but weight loss can be subtle. Perhaps you suspect a problem but the cat is so large to begin with that you aren't sure.

How can you tell whether your cat is losing weight? Watch to be sure your cat is eating. Weigh your cat once a week by weighing yourself, plus and minus kitty, on the bathroom scale. Some cats gain a pound or so each winter, losing it each summer. Unless your cat is on a diet, his weight should not fluctuate by more than a pound or two each season.

Cats that are too thin include strays that have been starved and cats on poor-quality cat food. Mother cats may lose weight when they nurse a lot of kittens. Female cats in heat may lose weight because they are more interested in romance than eating. But the major cause of weight loss is illness. If your cat is too thin or has lost weight, he should be examined by your vet.

Just about any illness can cause weight loss. Usually the cat must be sick for some time before he loses weight. Some diseases don't cause any other sign, so you may not notice anything else abnormal about your cat.

Many people think their cat has worms, and they purchase a dewormer at the store. Be aware, though, that there are several kinds of worms that can affect your cat. Each requires a different treatment. Your vet will do a microscopic exam of a fresh stool sample to find out what kind of parasites, if any, are present. A thorough physical exam and perhaps blood tests will reveal the reason for your cat's weight loss.

The best cure for weight loss that is not due to illness is to feed a good-quality *kitten* food free choice. Also consider feeding canned food, which may cause your cat to eat more because it tastes better. Avoid giving too many treats or just one kind of extra "people" food (eggs or tuna, for example). The cat needs a balanced diet. Feeding a lot of one kind of food will not "boost" the cat's health.

Skinny cats don't need extra vitamins since those are already in the cat food. When the cat eats more, she automatically takes in more vitamins. (See "Appetite Loss" for more tips.)

WHISKERS

Everyone knows about the cat's facial whiskers. But did you know that cats also have "whiskers" on their legs? Look on the back of your cat's forelegs, just above the paw. You should see a few long hairs sticking out.

What are a cat's whiskers for? Whiskers are tactile organs used for feeling. Cats feel wind currents on their whiskers. Whiskers help cats tell where objects are at night. Cats change the position of their whiskers when they are walking, sitting, or greeting another cat. The whiskers are held out as far as they will go when the cat is walking, but are held in close when greeting another cat.

Children sometimes cut off cats' whiskers as a prank. Even though it is not extremely harmful, it is best to discourage such behavior because it shows a general lack of respect for the cat. A cat without whiskers is not helpless, although she may need to depend more on vision and hearing while the whiskers grow back.

WILD CATS AS PETS

Imagine your friends found a mother cat and kittens in an old abandoned barn. They trapped them all and now they are looking for homes for the kittens. All the kittens are wild and do not allow themselves to be handled. But you would like to try adopting one. What's the first step?

It is tempting to imagine yourself taming a wild cat or kitten until the cat learns to love you. These cats aren't truly "wild," they are *feral,* which means they have descended from previously domesticated cats. But that doesn't mean they can easily revert back to being pets.

Review the information about socializing kittens in the section about adopting cats. It is important to realize that a wild kitten adopted at older than about eight weeks may never become comfortable around people. That's fine if you live alone or with one other person. It won't work if you have children or a large family. The cat may live in fear and never settle comfortably in your home.

So—you have decided to take on the challenge. First take the kitten to the veterinarian's for a checkup. That may be easier said than done. Try to lure the kitten into a small enclosure with food. If necessary, the vet can do a cursory exam without handling the cat. Then you can return for a more thorough checkup once the kitten has calmed down. Or the vet can give you a mild tranquilizer to put in some food shortly before your appointment.

Take your kitten home and keep her in just one room of the house. The best room is one inside the house without access to an outside door.

Although eventually you may choose to feed the cat free choice, give her meals for now to help her learn to accept you. Sit in the room with her while she eats. Don't try to approach the kitten. If she won't eat with you there, leave the food with

Barn cats raised without human contact may always be shy.

her, but gradually try to get her to eat in your presence. You may have to resort to using canned food at first. (Bribery does work.) Don't approach her while she eats; the goal is only to get her relaxed enough to eat while you are there.

Once the cat will eat in your presence, it is only a matter of time before she will approach you. Go slowly and let her make the first move. Try playing with her using a toy on a string so she can play without being too close. Take her some catnip. Talk to her all the time. Gradually she will become friendly.

What about true wild cats as pets? You may have seen tigers, ocelots, or other exotic cats pictured on television with their proud owners. Although their owners may be happy, the cats are not. No matter how cute, wild cats can injure you accidentally or purposefully. Wild cats should be left in the wild or in zoos where they receive proper care.

A domestic kitten can offer plenty of wild and fun behavior for anyone. To find the right "wild" kitten for you, go back to the beginning, "Adopting a Cat."

APPENDIX

CAT MAGAZINES

Cat Fancy
PO Box 52864
Boulder, CO 80322-2864

Cats
PO Box 420240
Palm Coast, FL 32142-0240

I Love Cats
PO Box 7013
Red Oak, IA 51591-0013

BOOKS

Medical, Genetic, and Behavioral Aspects of Purebred Cats
Ross Clark, DVM
Forum Publications, Inc.

1610-A Frederica Road
St. Simons Island, GA 31522

Pets R Permitted
Hotel & Motel Directory
Annenberg Communications Institute
PO Box 3930
Torrance, CA 90510-3930
    Extensive hotel/motel/ boarding kennel listings. Updated yearly.

Touring With Towser
Quaker Professional Services
Touring With Towser Dept.
585 Hawthorne Court
Galesburg, IL 61401
    Directory of hotels and motels that accommodate guests with pets.

SERVICES

Humane Society National Lost Pet Hotline
Report Found Pets: 1-800-755-8111
Report Lost Pets: 1-900-535-1515 (fee call)

P.A.W.S.E.
Solveig S. Foeley
RR 3 Box 972
Rindge, NH 03461
Nationwide personalized trip planning for you and your pets.

ASSOCIATIONS AND GROUPS

American Association of Feline Practitioners
Kristi Thomson, Executive Director
7007 Wyoming NE, Suite E3
Albuquerque, NM 87109
Veterinarians with a special interest in feline medicine.

American Boarding Kennels Association
4575 Galley Road, Suite 400A
Colorado Springs, CO 80915
Information about boarding and names of kennels in your area.

Cat Fancier's Association
1805 Atlantic Avenue, PO Box 1005
Manasquan, NJ 08736-0805
Source of information about purebred cats.

National Animal Poison Control Center
College of Veterinary Medicine
1220 VMBSB
2001 Lincoln Avenue
Urbana, IL 61801
Information about animal poisons. Sells a list of toxic and nontoxic plants. For help with a specific problem twenty-four hours a day, call 1-900-680-0000 (charged to your phone bill) or 1-800-548-2423 (credit card required).

National Association of Pet Sitters
1200 G ST NW, Suite 760
Washington, DC 20005
Information about hiring a pet-sitter; names of pet-sitters in your area.

INDEX

ABOUT THE AUTHOR

Carin A. Smith was raised near the small town of Reedsport, on the Oregon coast. She received her D.V.M. degree in 1984 after participating in the cooperative program between Oregon State and Washington State universities. Dr. Smith worked in Montana and New Mexico before settling into her present home in the mountains of central Washington. She lives with her husband, Jay, cats Wilma, Gumby, and Alvin, and two dogs. Her time is now divided between writing and relief veterinary work (*locum tenens*). Although her seven state licenses allow her to travel to some jobs, Dr. Smith usually works in Washington state. She is a regular contributor to the *Journal of the American Veterinary Medical Association* and was a contributing editor to *Cat Lovers* magazine. Her articles also appear in many other magazines and professional journals.